NEW POLITICAL ECONOMY

Edited by
Richard McIntyre
University of Rhode Island

A ROUTLEDGE SERIES

New Political Economy

Richard McIntyre, *General Editor*

New Deal Banking Reforms and Keynesian Welfare State Capitalism

Ellen D. Russell

Routledge
New York & London

Routledge
Taylor & Francis Group
270 Madison Avenue
New York, NY 10016

Routledge
Taylor & Francis Group
2 Park Square
Milton Park, Abingdon
Oxon OX14 4RN

© 2008 by Taylor & Francis Group, LLC
Routledge is an imprint of Taylor & Francis Group, an Informa business

10 9 8 7 6 5 4 3 2 1

International Standard Book Number-13: 978-0-415-95661-1 (Hardcover)

Library of Congress Cataloging-in-Publication Data

Russell, Ellen D.
   New Deal banking reforms and Keynesian welfare state capitalism / by Ellen D. Russell.
      p. cm.
   Includes bibliographical references and index.
   ISBN 0-415-95661-7
   1. Banks and banking--Government policy--United States--History. 2. Banking law--United States. I. Title.

HG2461.R87 2007
332.10973'09043--dc22   2007013957

Visit the Taylor & Francis Web site at
http://www.taylorandfrancis.com

and the Routledge Web site at
http://www.routledge.com

Contents

List of Figures

Acknowledgments

The writing of this book has been assisted by many more people than I can name. I am greatly appreciative of the wonderful department of economics at University of Massachusetts/Amherst—and all of the friends I've made there. It was indeed a rare and stimulating environment in which to think critically about political economy.

Steven Resnick and Rick Wolff have graciously spurred me to ask questions that had never previously occurred to me, and I am still digesting the ramifications of these questions.

Jane 'D' Arista has been graciously magnanimous in so very many ways. Jim Crotty has been very generous with his vast knowledge and perceptive insights. And to Julie Graham: my thanks for your support above the call of duty.

While preparing this book, I have benefited immensely from comments by Jerry Epstein, Lawrance Evans, Arjun Jayadev, Suresh Naidu and Jim Stanford. Marcelo Milan provided stupendous research assistance and commentary. Mathieu Dufour has been a constant source of joyful intellectual camaraderie and provocative insight.

I am very grateful to Richard McIntyre for his efforts on behalf of both my book and this important series of books. And to Benjamin Holtzman at Routledge: I am really greatly appreciative for your help throughout this process.

Thank you Kate Reynolds for, well, everything.

Chapter One

Finance As Servant?: New Deal Banking Reforms and Keynesian Welfare State Capitalism

AN INTRODUCTION TO THE "FINANCE-AS-SERVANT" PROPOSITION

Scholars of diverse theoretical proclivities contrast the increasingly hegemonic influence of contemporary finance with the relatively subservant role of finance during the era of Keynesian welfare state capitalism. Vigorous debates examine how this "financialization" (a term coined—although not defined—to suggest the pervasive influence of finance) creates objectionable economic consequences while inhibiting—and even foreclosing—the pursuit of economic alternatives.[1] Much research is emerging to document the many ways in which the finance's ascendancy creates objectionable economic consequences while inhibiting—and even foreclosing—economic alternatives.[1] In contrast to the ubiquity of finance's influence in contemporary neoliberal globalization, Keynesian welfare state capitalism has been characterized as an era in which finance was comparatively subdued. In this earlier epoch, finance is depicted as the "'servant' rather than the 'master' in economic and political matters" (Helleiner 1994, 5). While the pursuit of economic alternatives is not synonymous with the embrace of Keynesian welfare state capitalism, heterodox political economy has generally looked favorably on the "golden age" of welfare state capitalism for its vigorous economic growth, relative stability and reduced domestic inequality relative to contemporary norms (see Baker, Epstein and Pollin 1998, 18–19).[2] To the extent that the supportive role played by finance created space for the Keynesian economic reform agenda, the formulation of responses to financialization can benefit from a backward glance at the role of finance in Keynesian welfare state capitalism.

This book contributes to the reexamination of the role of financial regulation in the Keynesian welfare state. We consider the proposition that welfare state capitalism in the United States was predicated on finance acting as "servant" to the project of Keynesian economic reform, and analyze how domestic financial regulation created conditions conducive to this servitude of finance. This inquiry does not seek some way to replicate conditions of the past, nor to endorse Keynesian welfare state capitalism as the necessary goal of future alternative economic agendas. Rather, the goal is to perceive insights from this historical experience with financial regulation and economic reform that may prove useful to current debates concerning the possibilities—and limitations—of financial regulation as one aspect of a strategy to promote economic alternatives.

The story of financial regulation and the relative subservience of finance during the welfare state era has been frequently told in terms of the international financial architecture created by the Bretton Woods Agreement. In the words of the US Treasury Department's Henry Morgenthau, Bretton Woods is described as a "'New Deal in international economics' designed to curtail the power of the bankers at home and abroad" (in Helleiner 1994, 31). Thanks in large part to the influence of the Mundell-Fleming analysis of the "irreconcilable trinity,"[3] Bretton Woods has been viewed as supportive of Keynesian welfare state capitalism in that it enabled national governments to impose capital controls and thereby navigate this trilemma. "Insofar as [the Bretton Woods'] institutional structure reflected Keynesian theoretical concerns of the time, Bretton Woods may be interpreted as a set of rules under which national authorities might, if they wished, pursue full employment policies, free of some of the anxieties that accompany open capital markets" (Eatwell and Taylor 2000, 35). This extensive scholarship on the international dimensions of financial regulation during the welfare state has stimulated a vigorous debate over proposals for a new international financial framework.[4]

Relative to this extensive consideration of the international dimensions of financial regulation during the welfare state, scholarship on ways in which national (or subnational) financial regulatory structures supported the economic agenda of the welfare state is less developed. Certainly scholarship exists that speaks to various aspects of these issues,[5] but the interconnections between domestic financial architecture and the creation and sustainability of welfare state capitalism are perhaps more often asserted than systematically demonstrated. One legacy of this relative neglect of domestic financial issues in the analysis of the Keynesian welfare state is that contemporary debate concerning changes to domestic financial architecture that might support alternative economic agendas is relatively subdued in comparison to the vigorous discussion of international financial architecture. Hence, this re-examination of the domestic financial regulatory framework in the US hopes to stimulate the consideration of domestic financial reforms as one of the components of contemporary responses to neoliberal globalization.

DOMESTIC FINANCIAL ARCHITECTURE OF THE AMERICAN KEYNESIAN WELFARE STATE: THE LEGACY OF THE NEW DEAL

The American financial reforms that represent a paradigmatic shift comparable to the Bretton Woods Agreement took place during the New Deal. The New Deal is widely viewed as the precursor of many of the economic reforms that subsequently characterized welfare state capitalism. The various economic reforms of the New Deal will not be addressed, except to generally characterize these economic reforms as motivated to defend capitalism.[6] In the turbulent times of the Great Depression, there was significant concern among the advocates of capitalism that reforms were required to preempt the outright rejection of capitalism: "'We shall either adopt a plan that will meet the problem of unemployment under capitalism, or a plan will be adopted for us which will operate without capitalism'" warned Marriner Eccles, depression-era head of the Federal Reserve Board, in February of 1933 (in Hyman 1976, 106). Thus the analysis presented throughout this book is predicated on the assumption that the economic reform agenda of the New Deal did not dispute the continuation of capitalism *per se,* but was orientated towards economic reforms intended to ameliorate capitalism and/or enhance its viability. As is suggested in the words of Roosevelt:

> No one in the United States believes more firmly than I in the system of private business, private property and private profit. . . . If the Administration had had the slightest inclination to change that system, all that it would have had to do was to fold its hands and wait—let the system continue to default to itself and to the public. Instead . . . we acted quickly and drastically to save it. It was because of our belief in private enterprise that we acted quickly and drastically to save it (in Humphries 1970, 10–11).

Our focus is the financial reforms related to banking that were enacted early in the first Roosevelt presidency. We primarily examine the Banking Act of 1933 (although one provision of the Banking Act of 1935 is also discussed). While other financial reforms were later included in the New Deal,[7] the Banking Act of 1933 is arguably the most dramatic financial reform in US history, both because it created federal deposit insurance and because it restructured the financial sector via several of its subsections known as the Glass-Steagall Act.[8] Glass-Steagall prohibited the blending of commercial and investment banking, and this regulatory template for the "compartmentalization" of American finance persisted throughout the welfare state era. Thus despite the fact that these New Deal banking reforms predate the full articulation of Keynesianism (see below), the book examines the Glass-Steagall regulatory framework in terms of the ways in which this American domestic financial architecture was supportive of American Keynesian welfare state capitalism. Other countries had other domestic financial regulatory frameworks that responded to their particular contexts, thus the Glass-Steagall separation of commercial and investment banking is not presented here as the universal requirement for Keynesian welfare state capitalism. But if Bretton Woods is emblematic as the international financial regulatory framework that supported the Keynesian welfare state, I regard the Glass-Steagall Act as its domestic analogy in the American context.

Glass-Steagall, together with other regulations enacted in the Banking Act, presided over the so-called *"pax financus"* (Hayes 1978, 2), a long post-war period of relative stability in domestic finance that coincided with the golden age of welfare state capitalism. The financial sector is often characterized as having facilitated the welfare state, frequently via invocation of the metaphor of "finance-as-servant":

> The possibility of a capital-labor accord [during the welfare state] rested on the construction of a financial sector that would not be disruptive and would promote growth by financing industrial production. The labor peace achieved by the capital-labor accord required that financial capital act in a manner that was subservient to industrial capital. The New Deal constructed a regulated financial sector that was the handmaiden to industry (Isenberg 2000, 248).

The *pax financus* began to show signs of strain as finance increasingly rejected this servitude during the dénouement of American welfare state capitalism. Important aspects of this regulatory structure were eroded or dismantled in the 1970s and 1980s. In particular, the principle of financial compartmentalization came under increasing attack, until Glass-Steagall itself was repealed in 1999.

This book examines the banking regulatory structure that prevailed in the US during the heyday of Keynesian welfare state capitalism to entertain the question of how this domestic financial architecture created conditions that compelled finance to act as "servant" to the Keynesian economic reform agenda. Using this "finance-as-servant" perspective, we investigate the Glass-Steagall Act (as well as some of the accompanying regulations imposed in the Banking Act of 1933 and one aspect of the Banking Act of 1935) in order to consider the ways in which this regulatory framework was consistent with the subsequent creation and sustainability of Keynesian welfare state capitalism in the United States. We will build a case to argue that the attempt to compel finance to serve this project of economic reform embodies contradictions, and that these contradictions imply potentially divergent imperatives for the regulatory structure. By discerning these contradictions we generate a new perspective on the regulation that was obliged to navigate them. This facilitates a reinterpretation of both the ways in which this regulatory framework for banking supported Keynesian welfare state capitalism as well as the ways in which this financial reform set in motion tensions that ultimately undermined this regulatory framework and prepared the way for the contemporary ascendancy of finance.

This reexamination of the Glass-Steagall Act is timely in light of the intriguing similarities between the conditions that provoked the passage of New Deal banking reforms in the 1920s/1930s and a variety of controversies that have emerged in the 1990s/2000s. In the 1920s, as in the 1990s, exuberance about a "new era" of economic prosperity culminated in a stock market bubble. In both periods, stock market euphoria was accompanied by demands to dispense with the previous regulatory constraints on finance. In particular, there was intense and ultimately successful pressure on regulators to remove impediments to the combination of commercial and investment banking. Following the stock market decline in both the early 1930s and the early 2000s, the ensuing financial scandals were (in part) attributed to the various conflicts of interest that plague the combination of commercial and investment banking. This provoked debates about the desirability of financial reform, including a reconsideration of whether the combination of commercial and investment banking within financial conglomerates promotes destabilizing speculation and the misallocation of capital. Thus despite the profound differences in these historical periods, the similarities in these controversies that have emanated from the blending of commercial and investment banking invites a thorough consideration of the merits—and drawbacks—of the New Deal experience of financial reform.

KEYNESIAN ANALYTICS AND THE CONTRADICTORY IMPERATIVES OF NEW DEAL BANKING REFORM

This analysis is conducted with the assistance of Keynesian analytics, but the insights gleaned from this analysis are applied to a historical period—the New Deal—that predated the full development of Keynesian theory.

The General Theory of Employment, Interest, and Money was published in 1936, three years after the passage of the New Deal banking reforms that are the focus of this book. Our argument proceeds on the bases that the architects of the New Deal faced challenges discernable via Keynesian analytic tools, whether or not they were aware of these tools and self-consciously employed them to craft a regulatory framework intended to impose servitude on finance.

However, some ideas that will be identified here as "Keynesian" and employed in our subsequent analysis of the "finance-as-servant" question were in intellectual circulation prior to the publication of the *General Theory*. In addition to Keynes' earlier works, which anticipate some of the issues addressed in the *General Theory*, other theoretical traditions also offered analyses with affinities to Keynesianism. Critiques of free market capitalism were available via both Marxism (whose under-consumptionist theory shares some similarities to Keynesian concerns about insufficient aggregate demand)[9] and Institutionalism.[10] Economists of the time (such as Jacob Viner) and more contemporary commentators have argued that academic circles in the early 1930s were exhibiting the influence of ideas that in retrospect are associated with Keynesianism, despite the unfamiliarity of these economists with Keynes's work.[11] Some of the concrete Keynesian tools that are of service to the forthcoming argument were also known prior to *General Theory*. Keynes acknowledged that Federal Reserve officials were cognizant of the principles of counter-cyclical monetary policy in the 1920s,[12] and Keynes himself credited Kahn for a discussion of the multiplier in 1931.

Thus via theoretical cross-fertilization, empirical observation and practical experimentation, it is possible that New Dealers were aware of some the insights that are now associated with Keynesianism. Indeed, the claim was made that architects of the New Deal arrived at Keynesian ideas independently of Keynes. Mariner Eccles, chairman of the Federal Reserve in the 1930s, wrote of Roosevelt's Brains Trust:

> I doubt whether any of the men in my room had ever heard of John Maynard Keynes, the English economist who has frequently been referred to as the economic philosopher of the New Deal . . . The concepts I formulated, which have been called 'Keynesianism,' were not abstracted from his books, which I had never read.'" (in Mayer 2001, 158).

Whether or not the architects of New Deal banking reform were conscious of Keynesian analytics, we employ insights from Keynesian analysis because they illuminate many of the challenges faced by the architects of New Deal banking reform. (Indeed, Keynes wrote the General Theory as his theoretical response to the challenges evident in this historical period). While this explicit engagement with Keynesianism in the analysis of the early New Deal era risks some undertone of anachronism, it rewards us with greater clarity on the dilemmas of financial regulation in the context both Keynesian welfare state capitalism and in other potential economic reform projects.

Keynesianism suggests the possibility of economic reforms that may stabilize and ameliorate capitalism by enhancing aggregate demand conditions. While such a project of economic reform would have many desiderata, our focus is on those pertaining to finance. The Keynesian analysis of aggregate demand emphasizes the role of investment spending. While a firm that is deliberating over an investment project may finance that project via retained earnings, we examine the firm's access to externally provided sources of investment capital. Since financial intermediaries allocate the savings of an economy to its various uses, including the funding of investment projects, they have a critical role to play in promoting propitious investment conditions.

To the extent that the financial sector is compelled to support conditions consistent with vigorous investment, we may say that finance is the "servant" of a pro-investment agenda. The lower the price of investment capital,[13] the more opportune the aggregate demand conditions. The price of investment capital is determined by many factors, including market conditions generally and monetary policy. Since our focus is the financial regulatory framework as one among the many influences on the price of investment capital, we will pay particular attention to the impacts of financial regulation on the relationship between financial intermediaries supplying investment capital and firms seeking investment capital. A firm considering an investment project financed via external sources enters into a negotiation to determine the terms on which financial intermediaries will provide access to investment capital. The relative bargaining positions of the firm seeking investment capital and the financial intermediaries will exert an important influence on the price at which funds can be obtained. This book entertains the proposition that the banking reforms of the New Deal created competitive conditions among financial intermediaries that were supportive of the bargaining position of firms seeking an infusion of investment capital. To the extent that the New Deal financial regulatory framework thereby obliged finance to conduct itself in a manner consistent with making investment capital available on terms that were favorable to firms seeking investment capital,[14] we say that finance "served" the agenda of Keynesian welfare state capitalism.

The pro-investment agenda of Keynesian welfare state capitalism may have beneficial consequences for financial intermediaries. An environment that encourages the demand for investment capital is supportive of the profitability of financial intermediaries. As we shall argue below, the pro-investment agenda also requires stability in the financial sector, particularly among commercial banks. Since the profitability of commercial banks is the *sine qua non* of financial sector stability, the welfare state may be obliged to engage in regulatory or other actions that are supportive of commercial bank profitability directly or indirectly.

However, this pro-investment agenda is also potentially injurious to finance. *Ceterius paribus*, the profitability of financial intermediaries is squeezed if downward pressure is applied on the price they receive for providing access to investment capital. If financial intermediation is conducted for profit by capitalist firms,[15] and if finance is deleteriously affected by its status as "servant" a variety of consequences may ensue. For example, if constraints on the bargaining power of financial intermediaries produces downward pressure on their profitability, this may provoke instability within the financial system and undermine the broader conditions necessary for vigorous investment spending. Even if conditions are such that the profitability of financial intermediaries is sufficient to support stability in the financial system, financial intermediaries may still seek ways of incrementally subverting a regulatory framework which disadvantages them, thereby potentially eroding or even reversing the intended preferential bargaining position of firms seeking investment capital. Thus the pursuit of this "finance-as-servant" agenda must proceed with the awareness that to impose servitude on finance is potentially to set events in motion which may sabotage pro-investment desiderata.

While all types of financial intermediaries may be deleteriously affected by "serving' the Keynesian agenda for providing investment capital in terms that are favorable to investing firms, this book focuses on one particular actor in the financial sector: commercial banks. Because of the particular institutional characteristics of the commercial banking system, bank insolvency or instability may have consequences that undermine the stability of the banking system and create havoc throughout the economy. If a banking regulatory framework intended to support the pro-investment agenda of the Keynesian welfare state were to exert downward pressure on bank profitability, this situation might compromise the stability of the banking system. In this event, a destabilized commercial banking system could threaten the pursuit of vigorous aggregate demand growth. Commercial banks cannot "serve" the pro-investment agenda for economic growth and stability if their own instability provokes economic crisis. Hence any banking regulatory framework must safeguard bank profitability lest the pro-investment agenda be undermined by instability in the banking system. This consideration was very acute during the early 1930s, since banks profits were abysmal and the stability of the entire commercial banking system was in great peril. But the design of any financial regulation intended to support alternative economic agendas must consider the potential that any measures that constrain the profitability of banks and other financial intermediaries may provoke consequences that ultimately impair systemic financial stability and threaten the larger project of economic change.

The potentially antithetical tensions between the provision of investment capital on favorable terms and bank profitability oblige a banking regulatory framework seeking to promote investment to simultaneously pursue two contradictory imperatives. To enhance investment, the regulatory framework must promote conditions that support downward pressure on the costs of accessing investment capital while at the same time it must safeguard the profitability of banking. I present the case that the coherence of the New Deal's banking reforms is visible in light of the contradictory imperatives animating this financial reform. This regulatory framework configured the financial sector in a manner that was consistent with enhancing the bargaining power of firms seeking investment capital and constraining the bargaining power of financial intermediaries. But insofar as this regulatory framework potentially constrained the profitability of commercial banks it was problematic. Thus the New Deal banking reform was obliged to support the profitabilty of commercial banks in several respects, while attempting to do so in a manner that would avoid exerting any upward pressure on the costs of accessing investment capital.

The separation of commercial and investment banking was consistent with the creation of conditions conducive to the acquisition of investment capital on favorable terms. The compartmentalization of the financial sector, in which commercial banking, investment banking, insurance and so on were conducted within separate firms (nor was banking to be blended with industrial activities) stimulated competition among the providers of investment capital, thereby enhancing the bargaining power of firms seeking investment capital and exerting downward pressure on the cost of accessing investment capital. Yet Glass-Steagall was accompanied by other measures in the Banking Act of 1933. Deposit insurance and interest rate controls (as well as subsequent legislation that limited entry into banking) both stabilized the banking sector and supplemented its profitability. Taken together, these reforms sought to secure the potentially divergent objectives of promoting access to investment capital on terms that were favorable to firms considering investment projects, while also supporting the profitability of banking.

The emergence of *pax financus* during the golden age of Keynesian welfare state capitalism was enabled, in part, because of the dexterity with which New Deal banking reforms navigated these contradictory and sometimes entropic imperatives. This regulatory framework presided over a period of stable commercial bank profitability[16] in which bank failures became rather uncommon.[15] At the same time, the pro-investment orientation of the American version of Keynesian welfare state capitalism was supported by the low real interest rates (relative to current norms) that prevailed in the United States prior to the Volker shock in the early 1980s.[17]

However, the apparent success of the bank regulatory framework in balancing these potentially contradictory imperatives also contributed to the subversion of these reforms as welfare state capitalism proceeded. The compartmentalization of financial intermediaries necessarily bestows an uneven assortment of both special prerogatives and special disadvantages to financial firms of different regulatory categories. This creates incentives to subvert these categories. Firms of a given category seek to avoid the restrictions placed on their category while attaining the advantages enjoyed by firms in other regulatory categories. At the same time, firms in each category seek to maximize the advantages they enjoy under this framework while preventing any extension of their distinctive privileges to firms of other categories. These tensions may be latent under some circumstances, but the potential for internecine struggle inheres in a regulatory framework that necessarily creates an uneven patchwork of strictures and perquisites. Ultimately, the New Deal banking regulatory framework was undermined as conditions at the height of the welfare state set the stage for financial innovations designed to manipulate the mosaic of competitive advantages or disadvantages created by financial compartmentalization.

From this perspective, both the success and the ultimate dissolution of this regulatory framework is understood via the contradictory imperatives which animated it. In this sense, this financial history is at odds with many prominent narratives of the banking regulatory framework bequeathed by the New Deal to the post-war American economy. In the years in which the Glass-Steagall Act framework functioned reasonably well, and the traumas of the Great Depression were still keenly remembered, the compartmentalization of finance seemed an uncontroversial arrangement. As conditions evolved and the subversion of this framework gathered momentum, a new literature emerged which condemned Glass-Steagall as a gratuitous and perverse impediment to the efficiency of financial markets. This condemnation became so pervasive that one could be forgiven for wondering how a regulatory framework purported to lack virtually any defensible rationale could have persisted for so long.[18] The intention of this economic history is not to praise or condemn Glass-Steagall, but to discern the contradictory imperatives that animated Glass-Steagall and thereby to inform future projects of financial reform.

Progressives confront a US financial sector which has been substantially transformed since the days of the implementation of Glass-Steagall, but some themes recur. What are the economic implications of large financial conglomerates that engage in virtually all financial activities? What might the repercussions be if firms go beyond the combination of commercial banking, investment banking and other financial activities? For example, what might be the implications if firms such as Wal-Mart are allowed to acquire activities within banking (a possibility unfolding at the time of writing) or if online payment systems evolve to have attributes similar to depository banking? What sorts of difficulties might any of these financial activities pose for the state (particularly if these activities exacerbate the moral hazard dilemmas discussed in Chapter 3?). Alongside an international context which poses considerable obstacles to the implementation of progressive economic projects, these shifting domestic issues must also be considered as we contemplate the difficulties—as well as the opportunities—facing advocates of progressive economic change.

RECONSIDERING THE MASTER/SERVANT DICHOTOMY

This book invokes the "finance-as-servant" depiction advisedly. The use of the word "servant" is not intended to convey the impression of a static powerlessness. On the contrary, the intention is to understand financial dynamics from a more fluid and interdependent perspective. This analysis aspires to move away from a rather linear understanding of causality in which one force is the unambiguous master, one the powerless servant (or, mathematically, one variable is independent, the other is dependent) in favor of an understanding of mutually constitutivity in which all parts of a totality both shape and are shaped by each other. Borrowing from the work of Resnick and Wolff (1987) and others, the interaction among finance, production, the state, and other actors is understood as a ceaseless and contradictory process of interactive (and often unintended) effects.

Given this sensitivity to interactive and contradictory dynamics, we employ the phrase "finance-as-servant" with the intention to convey the dialectical sense in which master and servant (slave) are interdependent. As Hegel's master/slave dialectic reminds us, there is no possibility of mastery or servitude that is not subject to the negative moment of the dialectic (1977, 111–119). This dialectical awareness implies that the attempt to compel the submission of the servant also sets in motion its own negation. Context is, of course, important: the ways in which the master/slave dialectic unfolds will be shaped by (and in turn will shape) the context in which the master/servant relationship exists.

Any economic reform agenda hoping to compel finance to act as servant should anticipate the possibility that the servant may rebel. If finance is excessively disadvantaged by being obliged to serve the Keynesian proinvestment agenda, it might rebel in ways that would subvert the New Deal financial architecture, and thereby compromise the pro-investment agenda that finance was intended to serve. And given that the "finance-as-servant" agenda implies the subordination of a whole category of capitalist firms—financial intermediaries—in ways that may be detrimental to their profitability, these firms—*qua* capitalist firms—may have ample reason to rebel. Thus New Deal financial reformers were compelled to design banking regulations that navigated the contradictory imperatives of both constraining finance as "servant" while at the same time providing finance with sufficient benefits that it would acquiesce to this servitude. Ironically, if finance served the Keynesian welfare state agenda in some respects, it was also served by this same agenda in some respects.

Throughout this analysis, the description of New Deal reforms as "contradictory" intends the term "contradiction" to be understood in a manner that differs from that of common parlance. Frequently the description of an intervention as "contradictory" is intended as a rebuke, comparable to depicting that action as flawed or logically inconsistent. This suggests that some preferable course of action could be adopted that would be devoid of contradiction. My usage of the term "contradiction" intends no pejorative connotation. From the perspective of a mutually constitutive theory of causation, any policy intervention (or other economic event) is necessarily contradictory, in that any course of action will unleash multiple interactive effects that both promote and detract from its stated objective. No policy unambiguously succeeds—in other than a temporary and conditional way—in achieving its desired effect. A policy intervention may achieve some of its objectives within a specified time frame, but it also simultaneously sets dynamics in motion which reconfigure the status quo in uncertain ways that may ultimately undermine the initial policy intervention.

This emphasis on the contradictory imperatives that animate a dialectical perspective facilitates a retelling of US domestic financial history of this era. The pastiche of banking regulations that presided over the golden age of Keynesian welfare state capitalism have often been dismissed as an incoherent hodgepodge by their detractors. However, this emphasis on contradiction makes this regulatory framework intelligible as an attempt to manage divergent imperatives of simultaneously supporting and undermining finance. An awareness of the divergent impulses that animated New Deal banking reforms suggests that these reforms exhibit a coherent and even rather dexterous management of these potentially entropic tensions.

But at the same time that this analysis acknowledges the perils of navigating these contradictory impulses, we are alert to the persistence of the negative moment of the dialectic. Despite their considerable success, these New Deal banking reforms set in motion tensions that ultimately undermined this regulatory framework. By re-examining the inter-play of both the privileges and restrictions placed on finance, we can retell US domestic financial history of this era as the story of both the servitude of finance as well as its ultimate rebellion.

A NOTE TO READERS

The adherence to mutual constitutivity employed in this analysis compels me to acknowledge some caveats to the reader. Any analysis is necessarily partial, since only a subset of all possible influences can be considered. Thus this analysis foregrounds some factors, while leaving many others factors only tangentially mentioned or entirely unexamined. In the course of an analysis that spans from the latter part of the 1800s to 1999, the catalogue of important events, academic literature, and other germane information that has been neglected is vast. In earlier drafts of this book I included lengthy paragraphs to acknowledge important factors that I had set aside; I have elected to minimize these repetitive disclaimers. Suffice it to say that much is missing that might have added further interesting and important dimensions to the analysis presented below. My hope is that the value of the analysis that has been crafted with reference to a small number of factors will repay the readers' forbearance for the many factors that have been omitted.

This dilemma of what to include and what to exclude was particularly onerous as I contemplated the immense complexity the financial sector. The labyrinthine intricacies of various regulatory provisions and financial instruments often resists concise summary, as does the overview of the many salient events in the history of American finance. In an effort to generate a coherent, manageable and topical analysis of my "finance-as-servant" thematic, I have elected to impose certain simplifying assumptions concerning the activities of financial intermediaries. I opted for the clarity that these assumptions make possible despite the sacrifices required by their imposition. Where serviceable, I later return to these initial assumptions in order to relax them to some degree and entertain the new implications of these further nuances. But even if I had had the stamina to provide a book-length catalogue of endnotes to assess and qualify the omissions inherent in the imposition of these assumptions and the other simplifications that brevity required (and I do not have such stamina), the reader would still be required to tolerate the many instances in which simplicity and clarity prevailed over more profusive attempts to indicate the full complexity of the topics at hand.

My commitment to mutual constitutivity has caused me to experience some reluctance in including a number of graphs to illustrate several of the developments analyzed. My hesitation stems from the possibility that such graphs encourage anti-dialectical interpretation. Tidy graphs must necessarily exclude much more than they include, and can be constructed to confirm the author's argument while eclipsing the possiblity that any number of mitigating or exacerbating factors may have combined to produce the relationship illustrated in any given graph. Graphs have been included despite these reservations, and I ask the reader to view these graphs as provocative illustrations rather than conclusive summations.

The book is arranged in a manner that I hope will be helpful to both readers who seek generic lessons that are applicable to future financial regulatory reforms and readers who wish to delve into New Deal financial reforms *per se*. Chapter 2 begins with an exploration of the dilemmas of the "finance-as-servant" proposition via an analysis that largely abstracts from any historical and institutional context. It employs Keynesian analytics used to consider the contradictory imperatives faced by a pro-investment agenda, as well as Marxian insights concerning the nature of the negotiation between users of investment capital and financial intermediaries over the costs of accessing investment capital. Chapter 3 supplements this with some institutional considerations which prevailed at the time of the New Deal, many of which persist today. Beginning in Chapter 3 and continuing throughout the remainder of the book, the analysis is focused analysis on a financial intermediary with very particular institutional characteristics: the commercial bank. Chapter 4 provides some historical background to the banking system in the United States prior to the Great Depression, and considers the prevailing critiques offered in the early 1930s of the blending of commercial and investment banking that accelerated immediately prior to the stock market crash. Chapter 5 presents the New Deal banking regulations in light of the "finance-as-servant" analysis developed in the earlier chapters. Chapter 6 discusses of the decline of Glass-Steagall between the 1970s and 1999, with an emphasis on how the contradictory imperatives implicit in New Deal banking reform created incentives to subvert this regulatory framework as the Keynesian welfare state began its decline. The conclusion considers ways in which this analysis of New Deal banking reforms might inform contemporary debates about the pursuit of economic alternatives.

Chapter Two
The Contradictory Imperatives of the "Finance-As-Servant" Agenda

Architects of a financial regulatory framework seeking to compel finance to act as "servant" within a pro-investment agenda for economic reform face a number of challenging considerations. The regulatory framework cannot unambiguously disadvantage finance, as an undialectical usage of the term "servant" might suggest. If a financial regulatory framework attempts to promote investment via policies that disadvantage finance, the regulatory framework must also be accompanied by measures that are sufficiently beneficial to finance that the financial sector will acquiesce to these arrangements. If finance does not consider itself to be satisfactorily compensated for its role as "servant," finance may "rebel" from its servitude, in the sense of taking actions to support its interests that undermine the financial regulatory framework. Such actions on the part of finance could provoke consequences that are antithetical to the pro-investment agenda. Thus the "finance-as-servant" proposition implies contradictory tensions: the design of financial regulation must consider the possiblity that the promotion of a propitious climate for investment (via downward pressure on the price of investment capital) may also provoke conditions that are deleterious to investment (in the event that finance "rebels" from this arrangement in a manner that undermines the pro-investment agenda).

This chapter explores these dimensions of the "finance-as-servant" proposition via some of the basic tenets of Keynesian economic theory concerning the analysis of aggregate demand and the investment decision. We also draw upon Marxian theory to investigate one particular aspect of the relation between production and finance, namely the bargaining process that takes place between users and suppliers of investment capital. By employing insights from both theoretical traditions, we seek to outline the various imperatives facing the architects of pro-investment financial reform, and to discern ways in which these imperatives may conflict to some degree. This analysis foreshadows the ways in which the state may seek to manage these contradictory imperatives in its capacities as financial regulator. Finally we will also consider the ways in which the management of these contradictory imperatives constrains competition within the financial sector in some respects, while promotes it in other respects.

In the initial analysis of the contradictory imperatives inherent in the "finance-as-servant" proposition presented in this chapter, we proceed largely without reference to either the particular institutional complexion of the various actors within the financial sector or the particular historical context of the Great Depression and the New Deal. This lack of institutional and historical specificity is intentional: both this chapter and Chapter 3 are intended to provide an analytical framework that is relevant both to the retrospective analysis of New Deal banking reforms as well as the prospective analysis of future projects of financial reform. Thus the analysis presented in this chapter is conducted on sufficiently general terms that the insights garnered will be relevant in a variety of institutional and historical circumstances (although in a few instances I have been unable to resist mentioning a particularly illustrative historical or institutional detail). Chapter 3 will introduce the institutional specificities of commercial banks (although other financial sector firms will also be mentioned), and Chapter 4 will provide historical background relevant to the New Deal banking reforms. Historically and institutionally specific context will feature prominently in the remainder of the book.

KEYNESIAN ANALYTICS AND THE INVESTMENT DECISION

The analysis of aggregate demand put forward in Keynesian economic theory emphasizes the potential capriciousness of investment spending. Keynes rejected neoclassical economics' rather mechanistic view that underlying "fundamentals" govern investment behavior. While both neoclassical and Keynesian theory concur that investors consider the future rate of return on a proposed investment project, Keynesians believe that investors have no possibility of even calculating probabilistic information about it.[1] Confronted by an unknowable future, a firm considering the decision to invest must form expectations about the future profitability of alternative investment projects. The expectations formation process is informed by many diverse factors, including psychological and emotional proclivities, and socially determined conventions.

Via its analysis of the formation of expectations about the future profitability of investment projects in the context of fundamental uncertainty,

Keynesianism concurred with Marxism in the rejection of Say's Law. Both Keynesianism and Marxism contend that firms are reluctant to invest if they anticipate detrimental demand conditions. A negative self-reinforcing process can ensue in which weak or volatile aggregate demand contributes to instability in investment spending, while unstable or low investment exacerbates aggregate demand problems. The Keynesian ideal is to create a virtuous circle in which brisk and stable investment spending contributes to stabilizing aggregate demand at a level consistent with full-employment, while strong aggregate demand attenuates the volatility of investment. (Marxists diverge from Keynesians at this point, in the sense that Marxism understands aggregate demand issues as only one of many sources of instability within capitalism. Thus the pursuit of auspicious aggregate demand conditions may serve only to set other crisis tendencies in motion. For these and other reasons[2], Marxism repudiates the quest for stability within capitalism and seeks agendas for economic change that problematize capitalism *per se.*)

One of the necessary conditions of this virtuous circle described above is vigorous and stable investment spending. If a project of economic reform retains its commitment to capitalism—as did the New Deal and the subsequent Keynesian welfare state—it must contend with the implications of the fact that the investment decision remains in the hands of capitalist firms. An economic reform agenda attempting to enhance investment spending within a capitalist economy must consider the various ways to promote an environment which private capitalist firms deem favorable for the pursuit of new investment projects.[3] Our focus will be on one of the factors that shapes the investment decision of the firm: the accessibility and price of external sources of financing for investment projects.

What determines the price of investment capital? Both Keynesian and Marxian analyses suggest that the cost of accessing investment capital is influenced by a large variety of factors. These complexities are dismissed in any caricature of aggregate demand management that depicts the costs of investment capital as unproblematically governed by the manipulation of monetary policy. Certainly monetary policy plays a role in determining the price of investment capital, as do a large number of market forces that influence both the supply and demand sides of the market for investment capital. While our analysis of the price of investment capital acknowledges the importance of these factors, we do not analyze explicitly the influence of monetary policy as well as the entirety of the market conditions that shape the price of investment capital. Instead, we foreground the financial sector itself as it engages in the provision of investment capital, and ask: what financial sector characteristics might be consistent with the provision of investment capital on terms that are conducive to stimulating investment? Our ultimate aim is to consider what sort of domestic financial regulatory structure might enhance characteristics within the financial sector that are congruent with the provision of investment capital on terms that are conducive to the promotion of investment spending. Or, in other words, how might financial regulation compel the financial sector to act as "servant" to a pro-investment agenda?

BARGAINING OVER THE PRICE OF INVESTMENT CAPITAL AND THE MASTER/SERVANT CONTRADICTION

In any given context (with its prevailing monetary policy as well as other factors that shape expectations), a firm seeking an infusion of investment capital must negotiate with the supplier of those funds over the price of investment capital. This negotiation over the price of investment capital can be explored in Marxian terms, employing insights adopted from the class-analytic framework developed by Resnick and Wolff (1987). Based on a reading of *Capital* that emphasizes volumes 2 and 3, attention is focused on Marx's distinction between different types of capitalist firms: "productive capitalist firms" (those engaged in the production of goods and services) versus "financial capitalist firms" (firms that advance funds).[4] Our analysis focuses on the role of financial capitalist firms in advancing the investment capital that enables productive capitalist firms to enlarge their productive capacity.[5]

To facilitate our examination of the relationship between the productive capitalist firms in need of investment capital and financial intermediaries, certain simplifying assumptions are required. While firms may have internal sources of funds[6], our focus is on the provision of external sources of financing for investment projects.[7] In the following analysis, we will disallow the possibility that the funds provided to productive capitalist firms are used for purposes other than investment in productive captivity. Since our focus is on financial capitalist firms as providers of investment capital to productive capitalist firms, we will temporarily overlook the possibility that financial capitalist firms are providing funds to other entities (consumers, governments, foreign entities, etc.). It is assumed that all financial intermediaries are organized as capitalist firms motivated to enhance their profitability. We also assume that a financial capitalist firm is a financial intermediary[8], in that it collects the savings of the economy and allocates these savings among many potential users, including firms seeking investment capital. While our analysis emphasizes financial capitalists' access to funds via the intermediation process, it is possible that the financial capitalist firm may have access to funds through channels other than their role in financial intermediation.[9] In the case of commercial banks, the pool of funds that may be advanced as investment capital is not dependent solely on deposits, but is also affected by monetary policy and the possibility that it might have access to funds through sources other than deposits.[10]

These assumptions allow us to focus on the relationship between productive capitalist firms and financial capitalist firms in order to examine the size of the payment made in return for the provision of investment capital. In the third volume of *Capital,* Marx argues that the size of the payment made by the productive capitalist firm to the financial capitalist to secure access to investment capital is indeterminate.[11] As Resnick and Wolff (1987) point out, this interaction between productive and financial capitalist firms to determine the terms on which investment capital may be secured is the terrain of specific forms of inter-capitalist struggle.[12] A negotiation takes place between productive capitalists and financial capitalist firms over the terms on which investment capital may be accessed. This negotiation has an antagonistic dimension: productive capitalist firms wish to diminish the payment required to secure investment capital, while financial capitalist firms wish to increase it. However, the relationship between productive and financial capital also has a cooperative dimension.[13] Since borrowers need lenders, and lenders need borrowers[14], neither party wishes to make demands on the other which jeopardize the other's continued existence.

Based on this preliminary analysis of the negotiation over the terms on which investment capital may be accessed, we are in a position to clarify the characterization "finance-as-servant" used throughout this book. Finance—or more specifically financial capitalist firms—"serves" a pro-investment economic agenda if the situation is such that productive capitalist firms have more bargaining power than financial capitalist firms. If productive capitalist firms are advantaged in their bargaining position *vis-à-vis* financial capitalist firms, this is conducive to putting downward pressure on the price paid for access to investment capital.

This "finance-as-servant" situation is potentially injurious to financial capitalist firms *qua* capitalist firms, since downward pressure on the price of investment capital could undermine the profitability of financial capitalist firms. Because it potentially jeopardizes the well-being of the servant, the "finance-as-servant" agenda could be undermined by its own success. Finance will not be able to persist in this servitude if its profitability is so impaired that the servant's survival is threatened, or if it is sufficiently disadvantaged that it is provoked to take actions to resist this servitude. Since this contradiction between the agenda to lower the costs of accessing investment capital and financial capitalist profitability will be the focus of much attention, it merits a way of referring to it succinctly. We will refer to this as the "master/servant contradiction"—thereby acknowledging the debt to Hegel's master/slave dialectic. Prominent among our considerations is the possibility that, as Hegel reminds us, the act of compelling the servitude of one entity entails setting in motion the negation of that servitude.

There is no necessity that downward pressure on the price of investment capital must undermine the overall profitability of a financial capitalist firm. It may be the case that the payment for access to a given amount of investment capital decreases, but simultaneously the total demand for investment capital increases. In this event, it may be possible that the total revenue earned by the financial capitalist firms increases. Scenarios can be imagined in which a Keynesian pro-investment agenda may stimulate the demand for investment capital and create this result. Or, as we shall argue in subsequent chapters, it may be the case that the profitability of financial capitalist firms can be supplemented in ways that do not put upward pressure on the costs of accessing investment capital. But whether or not particular circumstances are such that this "finance-as-servant" agenda contributes to downward pressure on the profitability of financial capitalist firms, this potential is always latent.

Whether it is latent or overt, advocates of a pro-investment economic reform agenda must contend with the implications of this master/servant contradiction. Financial capitalists will not blithely acquiesce to a project of pro-investment economic reform if they anticipate the possibility that it will be detrimental their profitability. Any financial regulation designed to compel finance to "serve" this economic reform agenda will produce incentives for financial capitalist firms to undermine this regulatory framework to the extent that these regulatory constraints detract from their profitability. Thus financial reform intended to support aggregate demand by promoting the availability of investment capital on favorable terms confronts the possibility that by attempting to compel finance to act as "servant" of an economic reform project, it may also create conditions in which the servant may "rebel."

The possibility of downward pressure on the profitability of financial capitalist firms is not the sole consideration weighed by financial capitalists as they consider their support or opposition to a "finance-as-servant" agenda. It may be that a regulatory regime in which financial capitalist profitability is constrained is preferable to other alternatives. If a rival option is the nationalization of financial capitalist firms by the state, financial reforms that constrain financial capitalist profitability may be regarded as the lesser of two evils. Financial capitalist firms may even prefer a regulatory framework that promises lower but stable profitability to a situation in which financial capitalist firms realize higher profits on average but must contend with profitability that is more volatile. Arguably conditions at the height of the Great Depression may have been such that acquiescence to "servant" status on the part of financial capitalists was more attractive than some other potential alternatives. And perhaps financial capital was so chastened by the traumas of the 1930s that it continued to regard its "servant" status as an acceptable situation long after the events of the 1930s had passed.

But even if conditions are such that financial capitalist firms submit to the "finance-as-servant" agenda, this submission is always subject to reconsideration. Even a financial regulatory framework that has exhibited considerable success in navigating the master/servant contradiction may face growing opposition from financial capitalist firms as time passes and conditions are transformed. The passage of time and the evolution of circumstances make the previous crisis an increasingly distant memory. The regulations designed in response to that previous crisis may be viewed as increasingly and unnecessarily burdensome as the disciplinary impact of the previous crisis recedes, while the activities that had previously fallen into disfavor begin to be reevaluated. As Minsky (1982, 1986) reminds us, even stability may be destabilizing. Thus the possibility always exists that constraints on financial capitalist firms may become sufficiently disagreeable that financial capitalist firms begin to subvert them.

THE STATE AS REGULATOR AND THE "FINANCE-AS-SERVANT" AGENDA

Thus far the state has not been explicitly introduced into our analysis. Without attempting to provide any rigorous consideration of theories of the state, we note that the state is influenced by the interplay of a great number of forces[15], some of which compel the state to assume regulatory, supervisory and other roles that pertain to the financial sector. Our analysis will focus on the many ways that the state's regulatory roles shape intercapitalist struggles. Capitalist firms, individually or in alliance with others, join many other actors that attempt to prevail upon the state for favorable treatment (or to seek the imposition of unfavorable regulatory treatment on their rivals). Thus regulation implies a ceaseless process of action and response that continuously reconfigures competitive conditions. In part, this is acknowledged in the mainstream financial regulatory literature via Kane's description of the "regulatory dialectic":

This concept embodies an interpretive vision of cyclical interaction between political and economic pressures in regulated markets. It treats political processes of *regulation* and economic processes of regulatee avoidance as opposing forces that, like riders on a seesaw, adapt continually to each other. This alternating adaptation evolves as a series of lagged responses, with regulators and regulatees seeking to maximize their own objectives, conditional on how they perceive the opposing party to behave (1981, 355).

However, our consideration of the mutual constitutivity among more actors than merely the regulated and the regulator implies that Kane's seesaw metaphor is replaced by a much more multi-faceted interactive process. And given our perspective on contradiction, it further introduces the possiblity that regulation both constrains and enables (indeed a regulation that is a competitive benefit in some conjunctural circumstances may be transformed into a competitive liability as these circumstances evolve). Of particular importance to our analysis is the recognition that both productive and financial capitalist firms are cognizant of the possibility that financial regulation may shape their relative bargaining positions in the negotiation over access to investment capital.

Our analysis departs from the point at which the state has become persuaded—for whatever reasons—to embark on a program of economic reforms intended to promote the viability of capitalism in general, and that these reforms embrace the promotion of investment as one of their necessary conditions.[16] Let us say that the state is persuaded that finance must act as "servant" to this agenda, and the state endeavors to create conditions that are conducive to the provision of investment capital on terms that are favorable to productive capitalist firms. The state pursues this desideratum by enacting financial regulation that reconfigures the bargaining power between productive and financial capital, such that downward pressure is exerted on the price of investment capital. In this respect, the state enhances the position of productive capital to the potential detriment of the profitability of financial capital.

The "finance-as-servant" proposition could be understood undialectically as equivalent to a situation in which the state is "captured" by productive capital to the unambiguous detriment of financial capital. This "capture" metaphor suggests an unambiguous subordination of financial capital by an alliance between productive capital and the state that is inimical to our previous discussion of the master/servant dialectic in Chapter 1. While in certain circumstances the state may favor the interests of productive capital over financial capital, circumstances are perpetually shifting.

Any favoritism of productive capital over financial capital sets in motion the possibility that financial capital will rebel against these arrangements. Thus finance cannot be unequivocally disadvantaged. To the extent that the state enacts financial regulations that disadvantage financial capitalist firms, financial capital must be compensated for their role as servant to the state's broader economic agenda.

As Chapter 3 will discuss, the dilemmas of the "finance-as-servant" proposition are further complicated by the institutional context. For institutional reasons, the state has a distinctive relationship with a particular type of financial capitalist firm, the commercial bank. Any financial regulatory framework that impairs bank profitability could provoke a crisis among commercial banks that might jeopardize the orderly conduct of financial intermediation and overall economic stability. Thus the state has multiple reasons to concern itself with the profitability of this particular type of financial capitalist firm while it contemplates financial reforms that are intended to support a "finance-as-servant" agenda.

The "finance-as-servant" agenda implies that a financial regulatory framework must be designed that is supportive of productive capitalist firms (by exerting downward pressure on the costs of accessing investment capital) while at the same time supporting the profitability of financial capitalist firms in general and commercial banks in particular (in order to make this regulatory regime viable for the "servant"). In its regulatory interventions, the state is obliged to manage these contradictory imperatives. This is neither an unambiguous "capture" of the state nor does the state engage in an optimization problem of the type that is ubiquitous in mainstream economic analysis. This optimization approach would acknowledge that the "finance-as-servant" agenda must pursue two conflicting objectives (lowering the cost of investment capital alongside the necessity of securing sufficient financial capitalist profitability to avert the rebellion of finance). Faced with the two objectives, the economist might seek to select the right point in the trade-off between these objectives and designate this point as an "optimal" regulatory framework. Such a search for optimality overlooks the dialectical insistence that whatever accommodation is made will also set in motion the negation of this accommodation as productive capitalist firms, financial capitalist firms, and others react to and thus transform the "optimum." Our attempt is to preserve the precarious fluidity of dialectical interaction conveyed by the invocation of the phrase "finance-as-servant." In doing so, the state is understood as continuously managing objectives that may not be simply distinct and contrasting, but also potentially entropic and ceaselessly changing.

FINANCIAL REGULATION AND THE FINANCE-AS-SERVANT AGENDA: POTENTIAL RESPONSES BY FINANCIAL CAPITALIST FIRMS

Our focus on the price of investment capital emphasizes the relationship between productive capitalist and financial capitalist firms in the negotiation over the terms on which investment capital may be accessed. From the many potential factors that shape this negotiation, we will focus on the degree of competition among financial capitalist firms as suppliers of investment capital. The more vigorous the competition among financial capitalist firms, the more leverage productive capitalist firms have to bid down the price of investment capital. These competitive conditions amongst financial capitalist firms as suppliers of investment capital are also shaped by a large variety of factors, such as the number and relative size of productive and financial capitalist firms, the existence (or not) of barriers to the mobility of capital that impede competition among financial capitalist firms across jurisdictional boundaries, and so on.[17]

In the consideration of competitive conditions among financial capitalist firms, we draw attention to the fact that the infusion of investment capital from external sources may be secured in two forms: as debt capital (which requires repayment of the principal and interest) or equity capital (which requires no repayment but confers ownership in the issuing firm and includes the possibility—but not the necessity—that the shareholders will earn dividends and/or capital gains). Since the investment decision is made by comparing the costs and benefits of accessing investment capital in all of its forms, a project of economic reform seeking to promote investment will be concerned with the price of investment capital in its various forms. Thus this book will refer to the terms on which investment capital is accessed—and not merely the interest rate—as the relevant prices that inform the investment decision.

In the absence of any institutional considerations, such as differences in the tax treatment[18], we assume that debt and equity capital are generally close substitutes from the point of view of a firm requiring an external infusion of investment capital.[19] The productive capitalist firm in need of an external source of investment capital considers the costs and benefits of accessing both forms of investment capital. If the productive capitalist firm can alter its mix of debt and equity capital, it can enhance its ability to bargain over the cost of accessing both forms of investment capital. The simplest case of this possibility would obtain if the financial sector were organized in such a way that certain financial capitalist firms provide access to debt capital while other financial capitalist firms provided access to equity capital. In this situation, a productive capitalist firm could hope to provoke competition between providers of debt and equity capital, thereby exerting downward pressure on the costs of investment capital in both of its forms.

Let us consider the possible implications of a decision by advocates of a pro-investment economic reform agenda to regulate the financial sector in a manner that encourages competition amongst financial capitalist firms. Given the possibility that the stimulation of competition among financial capitalist firms as providers of investment capital translates into downward pressure on the profitability of financial capitalist firms, the design of this regulatory framework also needs to consider the master/servant contradiction discussed above. If this regulatory framework has adverse consequences for financial capitalist firms, it will provoke a response from financial capital. Authors of financial regulation need to tread carefully lest the response of financial capitalist firms subvert the intended purpose of the financial reform.

Basic tools of supply and demand would predict that the obvious response to a situation of depressed profitability among financial capitalist firms resulting from vigorous competition is exit from this line of business. The reduction in the number of firms supplying investment capital—notably mergers and acquisitions to produce larger surviving financial capitalist firms—can create conditions that are precisely the antithesis of the intention of a pro-investment economic reform. For if financial capitalist firms become larger and fewer in number, this enhances their bargaining power relative to the productive capitalist firms. This not only mitigates the downward pressure on the price of investment capital intended by the financial regulations, it conceivably could culminate in a reconfiguration of the financial sector that leaves productive capitalist firms in a bargaining position that is less advantageous than was the case prior to the implementation of the financial reform.

As Chapter 3 will argue, there are additional institutional considerations that financial regulators must consider in the event that their regulatory interventions provoke the exit of financial capitalist firms. The closure of firms that are engaged in financial intermediation—particularly commercial banks—has consequences that are potentially destabilizing to aggregate demand conditions. In this respect, financial capitalist firms are unlike productive capitalist firms because financial capitalist firms are financial intermediaries. The closure of the widget manufacturer made famous in the microeconomic analyses of perfect competition does not provoke the same destabilizing consequences as the closure of a bank. Thus the architects of financial regulation confront the dilemma that the exit of financial capitalist firms provoked by the stimulation of competition among financial capitalist firms may have consequences that are detrimental to general economic stability and are therefore injurious to the pro-investment project.

Financial capitalist firms have other options to enhance their profitability if the business of providing investment capital to productive capitalist firms becomes less lucrative.[20] As financial intermediaries, they may choose to allocate savings for purposes other than supporting investment (a possibility to which we return when the question of speculation is addressed more fully). Financial capitalist firms may allocate savings to other domestic entities (consumers, the state) or similar entities abroad. The provision of funds to these various entities may play a supportive role in stimulating domestic aggregate demand (as when loans are made to domestic consumers) or not (as when loans are made abroad for purchases other than exports from the home country). The possibility that a financial capitalist firm has other uses to which it can put its funds enhances its bargaining position vis-à-vis productive capitalist firms. Therefore, financial regulators may have multiple reasons to wish to deter financial capitalist firms from pursuing these other options to such an extent that it detracts excessively from the funds directed towards the provision of investment capital to domestic productive capitalist firms.

Financial capitalist firms that face declining profitability in the provision of investment capital can also consider earning income via capital gains. A financial capitalist firm may use funds at its disposal to acquire securities on secondary markets in the hope that their price will appreciate. The possibility of realizing capital gains has complex effects on the story told thus far concerning the price of investment capital. The possibility of capital gains is supportive of a pro-investment agenda in that shareholders and bondholders may be more sanguine about receiving low interest income or dividends if they are confident about the possibility of realizing capital gains. However, capital gains are a double-edged sword. It is possible that financial capitalist firms could relegate the provision of investment capital to a relatively minor role, necessary only to generate the securities which are required for trading on secondary markets. Moreover, the increased orientation of financial capitalists to the pursuit of capital gains may have destabilizing consequences in light of the Keynesian analysis of the role of uncertainty in the investment decision. One of the factors that shape expectations is movements in financial asset prices. An environment characterized by the aggressive pursuit of capital gains can exacerbate the volatility of financial asset prices.[21] This may provoke instability in expectations and further intensify the perils of embarking on investment projects.

This implies a contradictory attitude towards the pursuit of capital gains. The possibility of realizing capital gains can counteract the negative impact on financial capitalist firms of a downward pressure on the price of investment capital. However, Keynesians do not wish the pursuit of capital gains to dominate the conduct of financial intermediation to the extent that productive capitalist firms are made hostage to the vagaries of speculation in financial assets. Although Keynesians do not commit themselves on the precise point at which the pursuit of capital gains begins to undermine conditions conducive to the pro-investment agenda, the laudable situation (financial intermediation oriented primarily towards the promotion of investment) is usually distinguished from the undesirable situation (financial intermediation oriented toward capital gains in financial assets) by reference to Keynes' distinction between "speculation" and "enterprise." In the *General Theory*, Keynes contrasts "enterprise" or the "activity of long term investment concerned with the yield of assets over their whole life," with "speculation," or the attempt to garner profits by anticipating market psychology to take advantage of short-term fluctuations in prices (1973, 158–159).[22] It is interesting that the famous passage condemning speculation in the *General Theory* is followed by a less frequently quoted condemnation of the speculative proclivities of Wall Street:

> Speculators may do no harm as bubbles on a steady stream of enterprise. But the position is serious when enterprise becomes the bubble on a whirlpool of speculation. When the capital development of a country becomes a by-product of the activities of a casino, the job is likely to be ill-done. The measure of success attained by Wall Street, regarded as an institution of which the proper social purpose is to direct new investment into the most profitable channels in terms of future yield, cannot be claimed as one of the outstanding triumphs of laissez-faire capitalism—which is not surprising, if I am right in thinking that the best brains of Wall Street have been in fact directed towards a different object (1973, 159).

Keynes also acknowledged that speculation may provoke other developments that have damaging consequences for economic growth. Keynes' *Treatise on Money*, published in 1930, referred to the possibility that a central bank may seek to deter excessive speculation on financial markets by increasing interest rates in the attempt to reduce the flow of funds into speculative activities. Such a policy also increases the costs of investment capital. Keynes was persuaded that the Federal Reserve had taken this course of action during the late 1920s, and that this had put sufficient upward pressure on the costs of investment that it provoked the subsequent economic downturn:

> Nevertheless, the high market-rate of interest which, prior to the collapse, the Federal Reserve System in their effort to control the enthusiasm of the speculative crowd, caused to be enforced in the United States—and as a result of sympathetic self-protective action, in the rest of the world—played an essential part in bringing about the rapid collapse. For this punitive rate of interest could not be prevented from having its repercussion on the rate of new investment both in the United States and throughout the world, and was bound, therefore, to prelude an era of falling prices and business losses everywhere.
>
> Thus I attribute the slump of 1930 primarily to the deterrent effects on investment of the long period of dear money which preceded the stock-market collapse, and only secondarily to the collapse itself (Keynes 1930, 196).

These (and other) unintended consequences may be set in motion by making finance the "servant" of a pro-investment agenda. Financial capitalists may respond in ways that counteract the downward pressure on the costs of securing investment capital, or they may take actions that produce various types of instability that are detrimental to the aggregate demand conditions. Hence architects of financial reform are beset by paradoxes. Regulatory intervention seeking to lower the cost of investment capital may produce its own negation. Regulatory intervention seeking to stabilize aggregate demand may produce the contrary. The potential for these and other unintended consequences to thwart the project of pro-investment economic reform compels the architects of financial reforms to address the master/servant contradiction in hopes of mitigating the possibility that these financial reforms might subvert their intended purpose.

FORESHADOWING THE NAVIGATION OF THE MASTER/ SERVANT CONTRADICTION IN NEW DEAL FINANCIAL REGULATION

How might a state seeking to implement a pro-investment agenda enact financial regulations that navigate the master/servant contradiction? If the state's intention is to enact a financial regulatory framework that intensifies competition among financial capitalist firms in order to exert downward pressure on the cost of investment capital, it must also provide sufficient support to financial capitalist profitabilty, such that financial capitalists comply with their status as "servant" to this economic reform agenda. Thus so long as investment capital is provided by financial intermediaries that are capitalist firms,[23] the architects of financial reform must consider what might be done to support the profitability of financial capital in ways which do not impede the pro-investment agenda.

Financial capitalist firms are financial intermediaries, meaning that they access savings and channel these savings into investment and other uses. For convenience, in subsequent chapters we will refer to the collection of savings by financial intermediaries as the "first phase" of financial intermediation, and the provision of funds to their potential users as the "second phase" of financial intermediation.[24] The profit of a financial intermediary providing investment capital to a productive capitalist firm is a function of 1) the "spread" between the price paid to access funds and the price paid by the productive capitalist firm to access capital and 2) the volume of funds being intermediated. One consideration affecting the spread is risk. For example, a premium will be added to the interest rate paid on bank loans to reflect the banks' assessment of the likelihood that the loan will default. However, the volatility of profits increases as risk increases. Thus as financial intermediaries increase the risk associated with their activities in the second moment of financial intermediation, they may earn higher profits but they are more vulnerable to losses.[25] During particularly adverse circumstances, firms that have engaged in highly risky activities are more prone to insolvency than are more cautious firms.

The pro-investment agenda implies that the spread will be squeezed to the extent that downward pressure is exerted on the price the financial capitalist firm receives for providing investment capital. How might financial capitalist firms be compensated for this downward pressure on their profitability? While some appetite for risk on the part of financial capitalist firms is helpful to a pro-investment agenda,[26] the architects of pro-investment financial regulation will be loath to create a situation in which financial capitalist firms are induced to supplement their profitability by allocating funds to excessively risky uses, particularly insofar as these uses are conducive to speculation and financial instability. From the point of view of the pro-investment agenda, it may be preferable to mitigate any profitability squeeze that a pro-investment agenda implies for financial capitalist firms by supporting conditions which are favorable to financial capitalist profitability in the first phase of financial intermediation. If financial capitalist firms pay less to access the savings they intermediate, and/or they intermediate a larger volume of funds, their profit is supported. Thus financial regulation devised in support of the pro-investment agenda could attempt to counteract the downward pressure on profitability at the top end of the spread with other measures to enhance the profitability of financial capital at the bottom end of the spread.

How might financial regulation create conditions that lower the costs incurred by financial capitalist firms to attract funds? This can be accomplished overtly, as when rules are imposed that limit the rate of return that can be earned by savers who supply their funds to financial intermediaries. Another possibility is that financial capitalist firms could be subsidized in some manner to defray some of the costs of attracting funds. Still another consideration is the state of competition among financial intermediaries over access to savings. Vigorous competition among financial intermediaries tends to bid up the cost of acquiring the funds intermediated by the financial capitalist, thus exacerbating the "finance-as-servant" contradiction by further squeezing the profit of financial capitalists. We will argue in Chapter Five that New Deal banking reform was informed by all of these approaches.

CONCLUSION

Advocates of a pro-investment agenda face the prospect of designing a financial regulatory framework that navigates complex and potentially divergent imperatives. The desideratum of supporting the availability of investment capital at an advantageous price implies some favoritism of productive capital over financial capital. But the possibility of backlash implied by the master/servant contradiction obliges the state to consider measures that promote the profitability of financial capital. For this reason, the characterization of financial reforms as compelling finance to act as "servant" is somewhat incomplete and misleading, unless a dialectical understanding of the term "servant" is implied. If this is considered servitude, it is a servitude gilded by overt consideration of the welfare of the "servant."

This master/servant contradiction, and its entailments *vis-à-vis* the profitability of financial capital, implies that the financial regulatory framework will confront contradictory imperatives concerning competition among financial capitalists. The financial regulatory framework looks favorably upon competition among financial capitalist firms in their capacity as suppliers of investment capital. Yet out of concern for financial capitalist profitability, the regulatory framework has reason to dissuade competition among financial capitalist firms in the market to access the savings which financial capitalist firms intermediate. Thus pro-investment financial reform wrestles with the desire to promote competition among financial capitalists in one respect, while deterring it in another respect. As we shall argue in later chapters, this divergent agenda with respect to competition among financial capitalist firms compelled the architects of New Deal banking reform to create regulatory interventions in a way that navigated this contradiction.

Chapter Three

"Finance-As-Servant" and the Blending of Commercial and Investment Banking

THE DISTINCTIVE CHARACTERISTICS OF COMMERCIAL BANKS AND THE "FINANCE-AS-SERVANT" AGENDA

The analysis of financial reforms designed to promote a pro-investment agenda has thus far been conducted with reference to a generic financial capitalist firm. This chapter provides some institutional context to this discussion. We explore some of the ways in which the institutional specificities of different types of financial capitalist firms have implications for the design of a financial regulatory framework, particularly a regulatory framework that wrestles with the "finance-as-servant" proposition. As we shall see in subsequent chapters, the New Deal financial regulatory framework addressed these implications by separating commercial and investment banking via the Glass-Steagall Act. This "compartmentalization" of different types of financial capitalist firms became a prominent characteristic of the financial regulatory framework that prevailed throughout the "golden age" of Keynesian welfare state capitalism.

This chapter introduces the terminology of "types" or "categories" of financial capitalist activity to refer to the characteristic way in which financial capitalist firms access the savings of an economy. Each type of financial capitalist firm has a distinct manner of engaging in the first phase of financial intermediation: commercial banks secure funds by accepting savings and checking deposits (the US also has other depository institutions, such as "Savings and Loan Associations" which originally could only accept savings deposits and primarily engaged in residential mortgage lending); pension fund companies collect funds via pension fund contributions; insurance companies receive funds via insurance premiums[1]; and so on. (Investment banks have a unique way of intermediating funds, which will be described separately towards the end of the chapter.) Regardless of the manner in which they access savings, all financial capitalist firms earn a profit by intermediating funds, either for use as investment capital by productive capitalist firms or for other purposes. To simplify our analysis at present, we assume that financial capitalist firms conduct only one type of financial capitalist activity. Thus a firm called a "commercial bank" engages only in gathering savings via deposits and refrains from engaging in other types of financial capitalist activities connected with investment banking, the provision of insurance, and so on. At a later point in the chapter, we will discuss a "diversified financial capitalist firm," or a financial capitalist firm that engages in multiple types of financial capitalist activities.

Throughout the remainder of the book, our principal focus will be on commercial banks. At the time of the New Deal, and for several decades thereafter, commercial banks intermediated the majority of the nation's savings. Monetary policy is conveyed via banks; consequently, attempts to promote domestic investment can be frustrated if expansionary monetary policy is not adequately transmitted by the banking system. Moreover, because a commercial bank accepts deposits and clears checks, it has certain distinctive institutional characteristics that make it vulnerable to instability and create the possibility that this instability may spread throughout the commercial banking system. When the commercial banking system becomes unstable, devastating macroeconomic impacts can ensue, including the subversion of any intended stimulus in monetary policy. For these and other reasons, commercial banks are regarded as "special," and it has evolved that the relationship between the state and commercial banks has some unique attributes that have not typically characterized the relationships between other types of financial capitalist firms and the state.

This special relationship between commercial banks and the state informs the design of banking regulations intended to be supportive of a pro-investment economic reform. Chapter 2 made the case that the profitability of financial capitalist firms is potentially constrained by the "finance-as-servant" agenda. But there are specific difficulties that may ensue if commercial bank profitability is detrimentally affected by this agenda. Banks with weak profitability are more prone to failure, and bank failures have potential contagion effects that can endanger the stability of the commercial banking system. The destabilization of the banking system can provoke a vicious cycle in which adverse conditions for both aggregate demand in general and investment spending in particular are mutually reinforcing. Since a dysfunctional commercial banking system threatens to subvert the larger aspirations of the pro-investment economic reform, the architects of pro-investment financial reforms are obliged to pay particular attention to the profitabilty of commercial banks.

COMMERCIAL BANK FAILURES AND
THE PRO-INVESTMENT AGENDA

At this juncture of the analysis, we make several simplifying assumptions in order to explore the problems that commercial bank failures pose for a pro-investment agenda. We shall assume that commercial banks intermediate funds exclusively by accepting deposits.[2] Deposits are often (although not necessarily) attracted because commercial banks pay interest to depositors.[3] We shall also assume that commercial bank revenue is derived exclusively by making loans to various entities.[4] The assumption that commercial banks make only bank loans disallows the possibility that dividends or capital gains may be earned in commercial banking.[5] Thus at this stage in the analysis, commercial banks earn profit exclusively via the "spread": the difference between the interest received on loans and the interest paid on deposits (also known as "net interest income" in banking parlance). For the time being, we shall assume that there is no deposit insurance to reimburse depositors in the event of a bank failure.

Commercial banks are leveraged, in the sense that the total amount of loans extended is far in excess of the total amount of funds on deposit. The fact that a single dollar deposited in a bank supports multiple dollars in loans enhances bank profits: the higher the leverage, the more interest income can be earned from a given amount of deposits. While this leverage enhances banks' profits, it also makes banks vulnerable to instability. Banks suffer from a mismatch between the potentially short-term maturity of bank liabilities (deposits) and the longer-term maturity of bank assets (loans). Many deposits are payable on demand (see below), while loans are not liquidated so easily. This exposes banks to "liquidity risk," the possibility that a bank will have inadequate funds if depositors simultaneously withdraw their deposits in a "run on the bank." In the even that depositors lose confidence in the security of their deposits and a bank run ensues, a bank may fail regardless of its soundness prior to the panic of its depositors.

The vulnerability of commercial banks to bank runs is exacerbated because of speed with which depositors can withdraw funds held in deposits. This ready access has evolved in large part to facilitate transactions, since checks written on "demand deposits" can be used as a form of payment. Commercial banks have access to the payments system, a network which clears checks by ensuring that funds are withdrawn from and deposited to the appropriate bank accounts. However, the functioning of the payments system implies that delays in the ability of depositors to access these checkable deposits can not be tolerated. While other types of financial capitalist firms may also be leveraged, and thus potentially vulnerable to failure if savers retrieve their savings, commercial banks are uniquely vulnerable because demand deposits must be honored immediately at par. (For example, a highly leveraged pension fund is insulated from this kind of liquidity crisis if the savings placed in the pension fund may be accessed only when savers retire—a future event that can be predicted with considerable actuarial precision. A mutual fund may redeem its shares quickly, but there is no guarantee of how much the saver will receive as the mutual fund liquidates its positions.) Thus the characteristics that enable commercial banks to play their particular role in the payments system also make them more vulnerable to instability, and these same characteristics imply that instability within the commercial banking system may curtail transactions and thereby wreak havoc with aggregate demand conditions.

Banks are vulnerable to "bank runs," both because they have the capability of meeting only a small percentage of their depositors' withdrawals at any given time and because their role in the payments system requires them to honor withdrawals of demand deposits without delay. This gives depositors an incentive to withdraw their funds at the first suspicion that a bank's stability may be in question. Depositor panic thereby provokes the bank failure that depositors fear. Thus depositor confidence is the *conditio sine qua non* of bank stability.[6] Even a bank of questionable stability can survive so long as it retains the public's confidence and thereby avoids a bank run, while an otherwise solvent bank that loses the public's confidence could succumb to a bank run.

While retaining public confidence is of a paramount importance to every bank, individual banks cannot preserve this confidence unilaterally, regardless of the rectitude with which they conduct their affairs. Commercial banks are interconnected, in that the loans made by one bank become the deposits held by other banks, which funds further lending and deposits in still more banks. Because of these linkages among banks, failures may spread if the contraction in the deposits of a failed bank puts pressure on other banks to contract their deposits. This contagion effect can jeopardize banks that were not implicated in the difficulties that provoked the initial failure. Each bank has reason to fear any behavior on the part of its competitors that may provoke systemic instability, since a failure in an imprudent bank may punish prudent ones as well.[7] In this sense, the relationship among commercial banks contrasts sharply with competitive relationships among other capitalist firms. The bankruptcy of a competitor is regarded favorably by a productive capitalist firm, while the bankruptcy of a competing commercial bank is regarded somewhat ambiguously by remaining commercial banks, as it may lead to a bank run.[8]

Bank failures may provoke the antithesis of a Keynesian "virtuous" circle (see Chapter 2). Banks facing liquidity risk will refrain from extending new loans and will attempt to call in existing loans. This jeopardizes the ability of productive capitalist firms to secure new funds, and may even require borrowers to repay loans that under less turbulent circumstances would be renewed without hesitation. Bank failures also further diminish aggregate demand in that consumer spending declines as depositors lose their savings and the clearing of transactions is disrupted (in the absence of deposit insurance). As an economic downturn gathers momentum, loans fall into default, creating further pressure on banks. In a general economic downturn, the liquidation of all of the forms of collateral backing loans in default can create a general asset deflation.[9] In addition, any attempt to conduct Keynesian-style counter-cyclical monetary policy will be thwarted if instability in the banking system jeopardizes the reliable transmission of monetary policy.

In light of the potentially damaging consequences of instability in the commercial banking system, various regulatory mechanisms are designed to address the problem of bank failures (see below). Alongside these mechanisms, the profitability of commercial banking in general is an important requisite of a stable commercial banking system. Bank runs are discouraged to the extent that profitable banks inspire depositor confidence, and profitable banks are otherwise better-equipped to weather spikes in withdrawals. Moreover, as we shall see below, the state is anxious to avoid the possibility that an unprofitable bank may engage in desperate measures to enhance its profitability, thereby provoking instability within the whole system. In terms of its guardianship of the commercial banking system, the state would much prefer that commercial banks be sufficiently profitable so that they are both resilient during challenging circumstances and reluctant to act in a manner that provokes destabilizing ramifications in the system.

The institutional specificities of commercial banking add further considerations to the proposition that finance should act as a "servant" to a pro-investment agenda. If the pro-investment agenda succeeds in putting downward pressure on the costs of securing investment capital, this situation could be so injurious to bank profitability that it provokes a crisis in the commercial banking system. This crisis would not only jeopardize the viability of the "servant," but could create such destabilizing systemic repercussions that the economy would generally suffer. In that event, the pro-investment agenda would have subverted its intended purpose, since a stable banking system is important both as a source of investment capital for productive capitalist firms and as a bulwark of aggregate demand conditions more generally. Yet any attempt to enhance the profitability of commercial banks potentially runs afoul of the pro-investment agenda if the profitability of commercial banking is increased in a manner that puts upward pressure on the price of investment capital. Thus the specific institutional characteristics of commercial banks imply that the master/servant contradiction discussed in Chapter 2 has particularly complex ramifications that must be accounted for in the design of pro-investment banking reforms.

THE STATE AND COMMERCIAL BANKS

In words frequently used but perhaps most famously associated with former New York Federal Reserve President Gerald Corrigan, banks are "special" (1982, 2000).[10] The failure of other types of financial capitalist firms may produce severe economic disruptions, but other non-depository financial capitalist activities lack the particular institutional characteristics that compel the state to regard bank failures as a severe systemic threat. Thus it has evolved that the state is engaged in both proactive and reactive oversight of the banking system in order to buttress public confidence and systemic stability. Given that confidence in the banking system is secured not only by the actions of individual banks, but as a consequence of the perceived resiliency of the entire banking system, the state typically creates banking regulations (and conducts bank supervision) in an attempt to preempt bank behavior that might jeopardize systemic stability. For example, commercial banks are often prevented from extending a large percentage of their lending to a single borrower (or even a single industry), so that a crisis that emanates from a particular firm (or industry) does not compromise bank solvency.

But while banks are "special" in many ways, they are also capitalist firms. Like other capitalist firms, they are loath to accept constraints on their profitability. Moreover, they are engaged in competitive struggles with other financial capitalist firms both to attract funds in the first phase of financial intermediation and to provide funds in the second phase. However, the competitive strategies of commercial banks are shaped by the unique relationship they have with the state. As a consequence of the safeguards enacted by the state to enhance the stability of the commercial banking system, banks have both privileges and constraints that are not applicable to other types of financial capitalist firms. This assortment of both privileges and constraints has important consequences for the competitive strategies formulated by commercial banks.

One such safeguard of the stability of the commercial banking system that was important at the time of New Deal is reserve requirements.[11] In effect, the state legally obliges commercial banks to withhold a portion of their deposits as required reserves.[12] Required reserves reduce the degree to which commercial banks are leveraged, and can act as a source of funds to protect commercial banks from liquidity risk. In the United States, most required reserves are held in non-interest bearing accounts at the Federal Reserve.[13] Paradoxically, the existence of sizable required reserves may render them unnecessary. The perceived sufficiency of required reserves dissuades depositors from instigating a run on the bank (thus leaving the banks' reserves intact), while suspicions that required reserves are inadequate may trigger a bank run which forces the bank to deplete its reserves. While required reserves safeguard the stability of the commercial banking system in this respect, they represent funds that the bank cannot use to generate interest income. Because required reserves diminish commercial bank profitability, they are regarded as an implicit tax by commercial banks. Commercial banks are bitterly aware that other financial capitalist firms are not subjected to this constraint on their profitability.

In the event of a serious threat to the stability of the commercial banking system, the state is legally empowered to take certain actions designed to prevent bank panics. The central bank may act as a "lender of last resort" to commercial banks. Since the central bank stands ready to supply funds to commercial banks in distress, depositors are dissuaded from instigating bank runs. Access to this safety net further distinguishes commercial banks, since no other type of financial capitalist firm enjoys a legally enshrined mechanism of potential state support in the event of a crisis.[14] Thus lender of last resort support implies a competitive advantage of commercial banks over their non-bank financial capitalist competitors. Depositors[15] are willing to provide funds more cheaply to banks than to other types of financial capitalist firms to the extent that they perceive that the state is likely to prevent bank failure in the event of a crisis.[16] As we shall see in subsequent chapters, the possibility of access to lender of last resort support is taken into consideration by banks as they formulate their competitive strategies.

Ironically, the possibility of state support in the event of crisis may induce commercial banks to engage in activities that increase the risks of crises in the banking sector. Comforted by the possibility of lender of last resort support, commercial banks may migrate towards more risk than would be considered acceptable in the absence of a state-supported safety net. This "moral hazard" that animates the relationship between commercial banks and the state has the perverse result of creating incentives that encourage behavior on the part of commercial banks that the state seeks to avoid.

However, this moral hazard dilemma implicit in the lender of last resort support creates the possibility, but not the necessity, that banks will expose themselves to greater risks. Discretion is exercised over the decision to intervene with lender of last resort support, so banks cannot be certain that they will be assisted if their risky activities imperil their solvency.[17] State officials would prefer to maintain a posture of "constructive ambiguity", for uncertainty about the likelihood of access to lender of last resort support deters banks from the cavalier pursuit of destabilizing activities. When officials judge that a particular bank failure will not have unduly damaging ramifications for the commercial banking system as a whole, they may welcome bank failures as a deterrent to excessive risk-taking among other banks. Yet state officials are also fearful of tolerating such a failure lest it have unanticipated systemic repercussions. Consider the ambivalence evident in the comments of Paul Volker, former chairman of the Federal Reserve Board:

> The 1980s exposed various excesses which I think, to some degree, were becoming apparent in the 1970s. I can remember very clearly sitting in my office then, as President of the Federal Reserve Bank of New York, thinking that what this country needs is a first-class bank failure to teach us all a lesson—but please God, not in my District. When I went to Washington, I had the same feeling—we need a clear lesson from market discipline, but please dear God, not in my country. (in Mayer 2001, 101)

Since commercial banks cannot be assured that the state will intervene in any given commercial bank crisis, each bank must weigh the possible benefits of increasing the risk they assume against their assessment of the likelihood that state support will be forthcoming if the risky activity fails. Although the context of each particular commercial banking crisis is important, in general the larger the potential crisis, the more likely it is that state assistance will be forthcoming. Ironically, prominent commercial banks that provoke very large crises may be more assured of state protection, for the very magnitude of the crisis that their failure might generate makes them "too-big-to-fail." The term "too-big-to-fail" is frequently applied to banks of a large size relative to the commercial banking market, but it also may apply to smaller banks that have conducted their affairs in such a way that their failure puts the entire banking system in jeopardy.[18] Thus one of the perverse implications of the moral hazard dilemma is that it can encourage banks to increase risk in ways that are most disruptive for the commercial banking system, since any bank in crisis is more likely to receive support if its failure will provoke widespread crisis. For example, a bank facing immanent demise has an incentive to increase risks precipitously. If these risky strategies succeed, the bank may be able to earn its way out of difficulties; if the strategies fail, it is more likely to qualify as "too-big-to-fail."

Given this moral hazard problem, the state has a particularly complex relationship with commercial banks. As a consequence of the unique institutional attributes of depository banking, the state is compelled to provide stabilizing mechanisms (via the provision of lender of last resort support and, as Chapter 5 discusses, via the provision of deposit insurance). Yet these stabilizing mechanisms may induce behavior on the part of banks that increases their risk exposure and potentially destabilizes the commercial banking system. Ironically, the state's attempts to promote stability in the commercial banking system may, under a certain confluence of circumstances, provoke instability instead. If banks are sufficiently pleased with the status quo, they will not wantonly increase their risk exposure given the many downsides that such actions may have for them. However, if their profitability comes under pressure, banks' privileged access to a government-supported safety net might incline them to ameliorate their earnings by heightening their risk exposure.

This presents the state with further challenges as it considers the design of banking regulation congruent with the "finance-as-servant" proposition. In Chapter 2 it was argued that the proposition that finance must "serve" a pro-investment economic reform agenda must be considered in light of the possibility that such an arrangement may undermine the profitability of financial capitalist firms. But given the particular relationship between commercial banks and the state, the master/servant contradiction implies additional complexity. The particular institutional complexion of commercial banks is such that instability of the commercial banking system is particularly catastrophic for the economy. The potential responses of commercial banks to pressures on their profitability is additionally problematic given their particular characteristics and the institutional mechanisms the state creates to stabilize the commercial banking system. Thus the authors of a financial regulatory framework will be specially concerned to safeguard the profitability of commercial banks, lest any regulatory constraints that are judged to be overly burdensome on their profitability may provoke banks to act on the moral hazard implicit in the state provision of a safety net for commercial banking.

THE DIVERSIFIED FINANCIAL CAPITALIST FIRM AND "FINANCE-AS-SERVANT"

Thus far we have assumed that financial capitalist firms engage in only one type of financial capitalist activity: commercial banks only take deposits, pension funds only gather pension contributions, insurance companies only receive insurance premiums, and so on. We now consider the possibility that two or more financial capitalist activities may occur within a single firm. Henceforth, firms engaging in two or more financial capitalist activities will be referred to as "diversified financial capitalist firms." Our particular concern is a diversified financial capitalist firm that blends commercial and investment banking—sometimes known as a "universal bank." Since such firms were prohibited by the Glass-Steagall Act, it is important to understand how this type of diversified financial capitalist firm may interact with the "finance-as-servant" proposition in the context of pro-investment economic reforms. While any mixture of financial capitalist activities might occur within a diversified financial capitalist firm, Glass-Steagall specifically prohibited the blending of commercial and investment banking. Hence our analysis pays specific attention to diversified financial capitalist firms that engages in both commercial and investment banking.

Thus far we have not discussed the unique institutional characteristics of investment banking. Investment banks differ from other financial capitalist firms in terms of how they channel investment capital to productive capitalist firms. While banks provide loans, other financial capitalist firms may provide debt or equity capital by purchasing securities directly from a productive capitalist firm in a so-called "direct placement." However, the firm issuing securities may prefer to obtain the assistance of an investment bank to underwrite securities in order to reduce the risks and delays associated with selling its stocks or bonds. An investment bank can underwrite securities by purchasing the securities from the productive capitalist firm at a price below what the securities are expected to fetch when sold to the public. The productive capitalist firm receives its funds initially from the securities underwriter, and the underwriter hopes to recover this amount, plus some additional revenue in order to generate a profit, by reselling the securities.[19] In the interval between the purchase of securities and their retail sale, the underwriter is exposed to any change in market conditions that may reduce the market price of the securities. Thus in its capacities as an underwriter, the investment bank intermediates savings by matching firms issuing securities with the initial purchasers of those securities. In addition to its role in the provision of investment capital, an investment bank typically earns revenues dealing in securities on secondary markets, as well as through other activities.

These characteristics of an investment bank imply that investment banking is often directly and indirectly concerned with the pursuit of capital gains. In an environment in which capital gains are easily forthcoming, an underwriter faces a reduced risk that it will be unable to resell securities to the public at the required mark-up. Optimism about the likelihood of realizing capital gains will stimulate the demand for securities, thus encouraging productive capitalist firms to select this means of accessing investment capital. Moreover, many of the other forms of income that an investment bank typically generates are indirectly connected to the likelihood of earning capital gains.[20] The many impacts of capital gains on investment bank profitability exposes investment banks to the perilous downturns (as well as lucrative upturns) associated with volatility in securities markets.

The separation of depository banks from investment banks was a recurrent theme in the history of English banking theory and its subsequent development in the United States:[21] "Recognized banking authorities [in England] consider[ed] investment banking an inherently risky and speculative venture and, for that reason, considered any dealings in stocks and bonds an improper business pursuit for financial institutions entrusted with the savings of the general public" (Perkins 1971, 485). Commercial banks[22] were originally envisioned as providers of short-term loans for operating capital (since this creates an appropriate match between the longevity of banks' assets and liabilities).[23] However, throughout this book, we allow the possiblity that commercial banks may provide investment capital to productive capitalist firms, particularly since some productive capitalist firms are too small or are otherwise unable to access investment capital by selling securities.[24] Investment banks were intended to refrain from accepting deposits, and instead focused on providing longer-term investment capital via securities markets.

One of the major criticisms of the coexistence of investment banking and commercial banking within a single firm is the charge that investment banking priorities will influence the commercial bank's lending activities in ways that are deleterious to stability. Many such concerns were expressed in the hearings prior to the passage of the Glass-Steagall Act, but a sampling of these critiques will suffice.[25] Linkages between commercial and investment banking operations may encourage commercial banks to advance loans to finance the purchase securities (possibly with the securities themselves acting as collateral).[26] Investment banks may be better situated to attract underwriting business if they can lend funds to firms in the period prior to the issuance of securities. It is also possible (although often illegal) for a diversified financial capitalist firm to engage in "loan-tying" (making the availability of credit conditional on other business interactions). Loans might be made to the investment banking arm itself (or, if this is prohibited, less overt means of accomplishing the same thing may be devised) to finance the carrying of inventories of securities or to enable the investment bank to trade "on its own account" (to trade securities in pursuit of capital gains). There is also the temptation that the commercial banks' lending capacities may be used to advance questionable loans connected with investment banking business (for example, unattractive securities that an investment bank wants to remove from its inventory might be purchased by third parties with the assistance of a bank loan). A commercial bank may be less vigilant about the quality of its loans if it believes that it can use the investment bank's underwriting capabilities to enable its problem borrowers to issue securities and thereby repay their loans.

All of these ways in which commercial bank lending may be influenced by investment banking considerations are potentially problematic for bank solvency. If a bank's loan portfolio is heavily influenced by investment banking priorities, a crisis in securities markets could create a sudden upswing in non-performing loans. Moreover, the moral hazard dilemma implied by the government safety net for banks may interact with the conflicts of interest that animate the blending of commercial and investment banking to create further incentives for commercial banks to expose themselves to the vagaries of securities markets. In the event that problems in securities markets are transmitted to commercial banks, state officials may be obliged to broaden the so-called "narrow"[27] linkage between commercial banks and access to the safety net. During the tumultuous unfolding of a financial crisis, a diversified financial capitalist firm may succeed in misrepresenting a non-commercial banking crisis as one emanating from commercial banking activities. It is also possible that state officials may understand that the problems of a firm in distress are rooted in its investment banking activities, but they fear that the crisis within the firm as a whole may provoke contagion effects within the commercial banking system. To the extent that investment banking considerations expose commercial banks to the instabilities emanating from securities markets, the state may be compelled to regard entire securities markets as "too-big-to-fail."[28] Of course, internal firewalls and/or restrictions on the types of permissible corporate forms may be constructed to alleviate these conflicts of interest and insulate the banking system from these pressures. But such mechanisms are always in jeopardy if their breach opens lucrative opportunities for both synergies between the commercial and investment banking and new opportunities to impose upon the safety net.

In addition to concerns about the stability of the banking system, there are other reasons why a pro-investment agenda might frown upon diversified financial capitalist firms. To some extent, bank loans that support liquidity in securities markets serve the pro-investment imperative in the sense that conditions that facilitate the possibility of capital gains can compensate securities holders for lower dividends or interest payments (see Chapter 2). However, if a large part of the deposit base of the economy is channeled into financing activities within secondary markets for securities, this may promote a situation in which the whirlpool of speculation dominates "enterprise" (Keynes 1973, 159). Apart from the possibility that speculative activities by banks potentially compromise their stability, chapter 2 argued that speculative conditions in general can have repercussions that undermine investment conditions. Thus advocates of a pro-investment agenda who frown upon speculation may wish to constrain or abolish diversified financial capitalist firms as a way of both insulating the commercial banking system and deterring speculative excess.

Notwithstanding these considerations related to the stability of the banking system and speculation in general, our focus in subsequent chapters is on another way in which diversified financial capitalist firms relate to the "finance-as-servant" agenda. If a diversified financial capitalist firm is sufficiently large, it may enjoy a degree of monopsonistic power over the access to savings and/or a degree of monopolistic power over the provision of funds to productive capitalist firms. It is possible that a situation characterized by a small number of large diversified financial capitalist firms that enjoy considerable market power will give these firms some leverage over productive capitalist firms and may enable financial capitalist firms to put upward pressure on the cost of investment capital. This outcome is precisely the opposite of the one desired by pro-investment reformers. Of course, such a situation also carries with it its own negation. To the degree that a group of financial capitalist firms may hold market power in these respects, the incentive exists for new financial capitalist firms to enter the market in order to compete away this advantage, providing that market entry is feasible.

Diversified financial capitalist firms also affect the bargaining power of productive capitalist firms in another manner. Chapter 2 discussed the fact that investment capital may be forthcoming in either debt or equity form, thus a productive capitalist firm can gain leverage if it can substitute debt or equity capital gained via securities issuance for bank loans. To some extent, diversified financial capitalist firms can restrain competition among providers of investment capital, in that two arms of the same diversified financial capitalist firm are not likely to undercut each other to the advantage of the productive capitalist firm. There may be other considerations (such as a previous relationship between the productive capitalist firm and the financial capitalist firm that mitigates information problems) which also make it difficult for a productive capitalist firm to switch its business dealings once it has already established a reputation with a particular financial capitalist firm. If so, the productive capitalist firm could be compelled to issue securities via the investment banking arm of the diversified financial capitalist firm with which it conducts its commercial banking relationship, and thus lose any leverage that might be gained by having investment banks and commercial banks competing over the rate at which it can access investment capital.[29]

In an analysis of the relations between financial and productive capitalist firms, Hilferding considered the possibility that financial capitalist firms might dominate productive capitalist firms. His *Finance Capital*, first published in 1910, described a particular historical confluence of factors in pre World War 1 Germany in which large and diversified financial capitalist firms grew to dominate productive capitalist firms that were facing an acute need for large inflows of investment capital.[30] It is interesting to note that the financial capitalist firms of Hilferding's day were able to both provide loans and purchase shares.[31] Thus Hilferding argued that large financial capitalist firms were able to use their position as the gatekeepers to investment capital to maneuver into a position of dominance *vis-à-vis* productive capital in this historical and institutional context. This enabled financial capitalists to demand higher payment for access to investment capital and/ or other prerogatives such as seats on the board of directors of productive capitalist firms.

In the United States, Hilferding's concept of finance capital found its expression in the "money trust." These diversified financial capitalist firms, epitomized by J.P. Morgan and Company, blended debt and equity capital provision. The House of Morgan was one of the leading investment banks that had supported the development of the railroads[32], and the Morgan empire grew to have significant influence in commercial banking.[33] Morgans parlayed its extensive stock ownership and loan portfolio into 72 directorships in 47 of the largest US corporations, and thereby exerted considerable influence over both the path of development of productive capitalist activity[34] and on the payments reverting to Morgan and Company. Money trusts were increasingly objects of public hostility, as was evidenced in the analysis of the 1912 Pujo commission. The Pujo Commission described money trusts as

> (. . .) a community of interests between a few leaders of finance, created and held together through stock ownership, interlocking directorates, partnerships and joint account transactions, and other forms of domination over banks, trust companies, railroads and public searches and industrial corporations, which has resulted in great and rapidly growing concentration of the control of money and credit in the hands of these few men. (Meerschwam 1987, 68)

The size and diversity of their financial capitalist activities may enable diversified financial capitalist firms to enhance their bargaining power *vis-à-vis* productive capitalist firms, and thereby exert upward pressure on the costs of investment capital. Context is immensely important, for scenarios can be imagined in which the blending of various financial capitalist activities within diversified financial capitalist firms might facilitate investment. Many studies discuss the "bank-based" systems—in contrast to the Anglo-American "market-based" system—in contexts in which they have been supportive of investment.[35] For example, a highly interventionist state may eschew the allocation of investment capital via market forces and force financial intermediaries to support a state-orchestrated development strategy. In this event, diversified financial capitalist firms might act as a powerful conduit for pro-investment public policy.[36] Other characteristics of diversified financial capitalist firms, such as their size and number relative to productive capitalist firms, will also shape their bargaining power with respect to the latter. Many aspects of financial regulation, such as any jurisdictional barriers to the operations of financial capitalist firms, will also influence their relative bargaining power.

Up to this point, we have assumed that diversified financial capitalist firms engage only in the full spectrum of financial capitalist activities and are excluded from participating in other types of capitalist activities. If we were to relax this assumption to consider the possiblity that diversified financial capitalist firms are permitted to expand into productive capitalist activities (or vice versa), our previous characterization of the relationships between productive and financial capital would have to be substantially revised. Once a firm acts as both a productive capitalist firm that uses investment capital to finance production and a financial capitalist firm that supplies investment capital to productive capitalist firms, the "arm's length" relationship we have assumed among participants in the market for investment capital no longer holds. Thus the character of the negotiation over access to investment capital will be transformed. We will return to this possiblity in the latter part of the book, where we will call a firm that mixes productive and financial capitalist activities a "diversified capitalist firm." However, for the majority of the book, we will preserve a clear separation between productive capitalist firms and financial capitalist firms.

Our prevailing concern is that contextual circumstances will be such that diversified financial capitalist firms may be an anathema to a pro-investment agenda of economic reform. If conditions are such that diversified financial capitalist firms are better situated to shift bargaining power away from productive capitalist firms, then diversified financial capitalist firms are antithetical to the "finance-as-servant" proposition. Moreover, since multiple financial capitalist activities are open to diversified financial capitalist firms, this may provide them with increased latitude to resist or subvert any "servitude" imposed upon them. Thus architects of a financial regulatory structure intended to support a pro-investment economic reform agenda may have ample reason to disapprove of diversified financial capitalist firms. Fears that they could contribute to speculation and bank stability, as well as the desire to promote the "finance-as-servant" agenda, may coincide in the denunciation of diversified financial capitalist firms.

Chapter Four

Prelude to the 1930s: The Rise and Repudiation of Commercial Bank Participation in Investment Banking

Thus far we have discussed the "finance-as-servant" proposition and its relationship to the blending of commercial and investment banking with minimal reference to the historical and institutional context of the US financial sector prior to the passage of the New Deal banking reforms. From the many years of financial history that preceded the 1930s and the many complex institutional considerations that the distinguish American financial sector, this chapter highlights a few factors that informed New Dealers decision to make the separation of commercial and investment banking the centerpiece of their financial reform project.

After a somewhat tumultuous history,[1] commercial banking system entered the 1920s exhibiting signs of strain. As the stock market flourished, commercial banks chafed at the regulatory restrictions that prevented them from full participation in activities related to the stock market. Remaining restrictions to commercial bank entry into investment banking were removed by the passage of the McFadden Act in 1927, and a heady period of mergers and acquisitions followed which enabled commercial banks to establish a substantial presence in investment banking.

Following the stock market crash and the onset of the Great Depression, the debilitating of the banking crises of the early 1930s provoked renewed scrutiny of the decision to permit commercial bank participation in investment banking. By 1933, it was widely argued that the blending of commercial and investment banking during the stock market boom contributed to the speculative excesses of the 1920s and planted the seeds of bank instability that would come to fruition during the early 1930s. The increasing influence of this critique led to the passage of the Glass-Steagall Act's prohibition on the blending of commercial and investment banking as a prominent part of the New Deal banking reforms of 1933.

US COMMERCIAL BANKING PRIOR TO THE 1930S

One of the distinctive aspects of commercial banking in the United States has been the relatively large number of commercial banks in operation. This profusion of commercial banks was in part a reaction against the bank chartering process of the late 1700s and early 1800s. At that time a special legislative act was required to permit entry into commercial banking. This element of discretion afforded officials the opportunity to demand financial or political favors in return for permission to open a bank. In response, critics embraced "free banking," meaning the ability of any firm to enter commercial banking so long as it satisfied certain rather minimal general conditions that were uniformly applied to all market entrants. In 1838 the state of New York passed the Free Banking Act, and ultimately the principle of free banking was enshrined by many states and in the National Banking Act of 1863. Until free banking was abandoned by the New Deal banking reforms, this policy of relative ease of entry into commercial banking

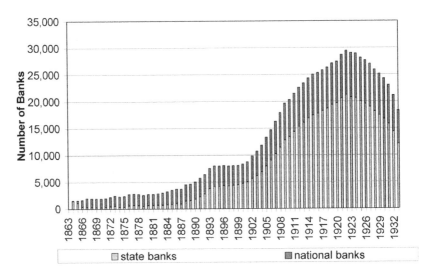

Figure 1. Number of Incorporated Commercial Banks, 1863–1932.

Source: Banking Studies.

helped to create the large number of firms in the US commercial banking system (see Figure 1).[2]

By the 1930s, the principle of free banking had fallen into disfavor. Free banking had often been accompanied by lenient capital requirements in order to encourage market entry. Thus from the perspective of the 1930s, free banking was viewed as contributing to dubious bank solvency and sometimes notorious banking practices.[3] Given the institutional characteristics that make possible the contagion effects of bank failures, the ease with which under-capitalized banks could enter banking and subsequently imperil the stability of the banking system was troubling to New Deal reformers. Parker Willis, who was prominent in the 1930s as an advisor to Carter Glass and vocal proponent of the Glass-Steagall Act, co-edited an extensive study of the "banking problem" with John Chapman and offered this summation:

> Charters were granted frequently with little or no regard to the qualifications of the applicants. In many cases the men running these banks knew little about the principles and practices of banking. Many of the new banks were not only foredoomed to failure but were also likely to imperil the existence of other banking institutions. The establishment of such large number of small banks has in itself presented many problems, the principal of which are the difficulties of making adequate earnings, of providing reasonably competent management, and the inherent difficulties of exercising proper supervision over a large number of small institutions (Willis, 1934b, 198).[4]

In addition to free banking, other regulatory peculiarities also encouraged the large number of rather leniently regulated commercial banks. The United States has a dual banking system, in that commercial banks may be organized at the state or national level. This creates multiple regulatory structures, with the Office of the Comptroller of the Currency (OCC) regulating national commercial banks and various state authorities (and the Federal Reserve to various extents over time) regulating state banks. This fragmented regulatory environment contributed to the proliferation of commercial banks. Regulatory agencies compete with each other to charter and regulate commercial banks. Competitive chartering provides banks with the opportunity to threaten to change the jurisdiction in which they are chartered in order to compel regulators to match or exceed the permissiveness of rival jurisdictions. Regulators may be compelled to engage in this competition for a variety of reasons, including the possiblity that their jurisdictions may earn great revenues as a consequence of chartering more banks.[5] Competition to charter banks produced what F. G. Awalt, acting Comptroller of the Currency, described in 1932 as a "competition in laxity" (in Wheelock 1992, 6).[6]

Jurisdictional tensions among the multiple regulatory authorities are also infused with a variety of other competitive struggles. For example, a local bank may fear competition from a state-wide bank, while a state-wide bank may fear competition from out-of-state banks. Local and regional banks' advocates have often found common cause with regional manufacturing and farming interests in stimulating hostility to out-of-state banks or even "big-city" banks. These interests contributed to a veneration of local banking[7] that made restrictions disadvantaging banks from other jurisdictions politically popular. Hence, during much of US banking history there have been limitations on the geographic scope of bank activities, such as limits on interstate banking, constraints on branching, and even "unit" banking (the prohibition on branching). These regulatory impediments to the geographic location of banks contributed to the large number of commercial banks in operation, and implicitly restrained the overall size of banks. The resistance to nation-wide banking has had both stabilizing and destabilizing consequences. Smaller banks, with geographically concentrated depositors and lending portfolios, are more easily destabilized by local economic difficulties.[8] However, barriers to nation-wide banking do provide some impediments to the transmission of bank instability across jurisdictional boundaries.

Between the turn of the century and 1920, the number of incorporated banks grew from 8,320 to 28,695 (see Figure 1). Thereafter, the number of banks began to decline, due in part to the upward trend of bank failure rates in the 1920s.[9] In this context, the term "over-banking" was coined to refer to the intense competition in a crowded commercial banking market.[10] For example, Wheelock states that North Dakota had 1.4 banks per 1000 inhabitants in 1920 (1992, 3). In their retrospective examinations of events that contributed to the crisis in commercial banking during the Great Depression, many regulatory authorities became convinced that over-banking had contributed to the instability within the US commercial banking system. New Deal era commentators argued that the competitive pressures generated by over-banking had squeezed the profitability of commercial banks and enticed them to migrate towards heightened risks to enhance their profitability. J.F.T. O'Connor, a prominent financial regulator privy to the high level policy debates of the New Deal era,[11] produced an analysis of the banking crisis of the 1930s in which he claimed that the ease of entry into commercial banking had created a situation in which "[b]anks became too numerous; competition too great; necessity for profit too urgent" (1938, 7). These highly competitive conditions eroded profits in both phases of financial intermediation, as a report of a survey of banking conditions in Indiana illustrates:

> Competition for deposits drove interest rates up to fantastic figures and resulted in all types of free services being offered. Competition for loans was so great that conservative credit principles were abandoned in an effort to secure business. (. . .) Exhaustive studies that have been made on this subject all agree that the over-banked condition of the state was, in a considerable measure, responsible, both directly and indirectly, for the large number of failures which occurred among banks in Indiana in the decade of the '20's and in the early '30's (O'Connor 1938, 85).

BANKS AND THE STOCK MARKET BOOM OF THE 1920s

The increasingly prominent role of the stock market during the 1920s had important consequences for commercial banks. Prior to the 1920s, accessing investment capital provided in securities markets was not a viable option for many productive capitalist firms. As securities markets flourished in the 1920s, more productive capitalist firms were able to access investment capital by issuing securities. And with the conclusion of the First World War and the arrival of economic prosperity in the 1920s, the American public became increasingly enthusiastic purchasers of securities.[12] Investment banks were well situated to benefit both from the appetite of firms seeking to raise funds via securities offerings and the desire of the public to purchase securities. During the 1920s, there ensued a "mad scramble" (Edwards 1938, 230) to enter investment banking activities. With new investment banks willing to do business with a greater variety of productive capitalist firms and ready demand for corporate securities, the offerings of these instruments mushroomed (see Figure 2). A "new era" had arrived in the 1920s in which:

> corporations came more and more to avoid borrowing at banks, and to substitute therefore the practice of providing themselves with working capital in the stock market. (. . .) This new era was to be one in which the business enterprise would no longer be dependent upon the bank and would resort to the public in order to satisfy its needs for capital (Willis, 1934a, 35).

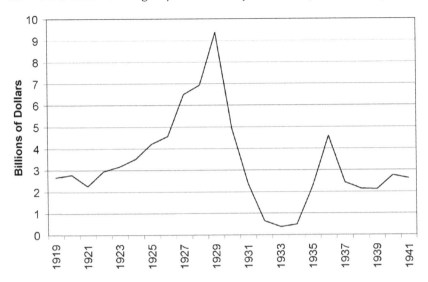

Figure 2. Corporate Securities Offerings, 1919–1941.

Source: Banking and Monetary Statistics.

As Chapter 3 argued, the ability of productive capitalist firms to access funds by means other than bank loans increases their bargaining power relative to financial capitalist firms. To the extent that securities issuance became more accessible, the bargaining power of productive capitalist firms was enhanced. Thus the capacity to rely on securities issuance (and retained earnings) gave productive capitalist firms the wherewithal to turn away from their commercial bankers:[13]

> After 1919, corporations of all types, not just railroads and heavy industries, discovered an American public, now committed to the investing habit, very receptive to new securities issues of unprecedented frequency and dollar volume. As a consequence of this new access to the supply of long-term capital, many companies found they were far less reliant on banks to provide short-term, seasonal financing. In addition, high profits gave many corporations such a large cash flow that outside borrowing was unnecessary (Perkins 1971, 493).

Under these circumstances, the "decline of the commercial loan" was heralded in the pages of the *Quarterly Journal of Economics* by Lauchlin Currie in 1931. Currie reported that commercial loans expressed as a percentage of the total earning assets of national banks declined from 57.5

percent in 1920 to 37 percent in 1929.[14] It would be instructive to compare the total value of bank loans to productive capitalist firms with the securities issued by productive capitalist firms during this period, but (to my knowledge) only a partial indication of this is possible given the limitations of the data available. Securities issued by productive capitalist firms are approximated in Figure 3.[15] Ascertaining the total amount of commercial bank loans to productive capitalist firms over this period is highly problematic, given the multiple jurisdictions of banks and the limited statistics produced by these various regulatory authorities. Figure 3 refers only to loans advanced by Federal Reserve member banks for purposes unconnected with dealings in securities,[16] and compares these loans to the dollar value of securities issued.

As the 1920s progressed, commercial banks were plagued both by over-banking and competition from investment banks (and trust companies[17]). In addition, bankers complained about other banking regulations that were increasingly disadvantageous in these particular circumstances.[18] In contrast to the challenging conditions that prevailed in commercial banking, profitable opportunities associated with the booming stock market were enticing. As Melvin Traylor of First National Bank of Chicago testified: "In the purely banking business, where you accept deposits and

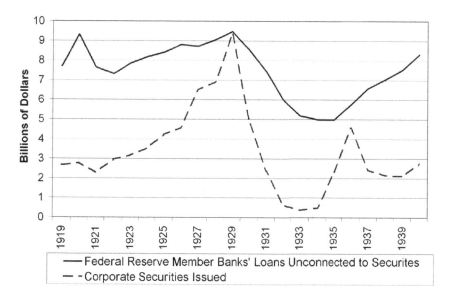

Figure 3. Corporate Securities Offerings, 1919–1941.

Source: Banking and Monetary Statistics.

make loans, the pickings, in the language of the street, got short and that led to the development of the trust business and security business (. . .)" (in Peach 1941, 25 fn). Commercial banks responded to these circumstances by seeking entry into investment banking:

> This decline in loan demand threatened the earning power of commercial banks and encouraged them to seek other opportunities for profit. An expansion of investment banking functions to offset the reduction in loan revenues was a course chosen by more and more large urban institutions (Perkins 1971, 493).

Commercial banks had previously attempted to expand into securities underwriting via their bond departments, but these attempts were curtailed by the regulator of the nationally-chartered commercial banks, the Comptroller of the Currency (Carosso 1970, 97).[19] Commercial banks attempted to circumvent these restrictions via securities affiliates, but the growth of these securities affiliates was constrained because of legal disputes, regulatory uncertainties, and potential anti-trust concerns. By the mid-1920s, many state jurisdictions were becoming increasingly permissive in allowing state-chartered commercial banks to migrate into investment banking activities. In 1927, the remaining obstacles were surmounted by the passage of the McFadden Act, which enabled nationally-chartered banks to fully engage in securities underwriting via the creation of securities affiliates. (The McFadden Act is perhaps more often remembered for its prevention of bank expansion across state lines, thereby contributing to the perpetuation of the over-banking dilemma.)

The passage of the McFadden Act marked the full-scale regulatory embrace of diversified financial capitalist firms that blended commercial and investment banking. A surge of mergers among commercial banks and free-standing investment banks followed the passage of the McFadden Act, and by 1929 nearly every large urban commercial bank had one or more securities affiliates (Carosso 1970, 278). These new securities affiliates quickly grew to be a formidable presence in the investment banking field. Among nationally-chartered commercial banks, Peach reports that commercial bank-related underwriters[20] issued 22 percent of all new bonds in 1927, while by 1929 they had 45.5 percent of the share of total bond issues (1941, 109).

THE BANKING CRISIS OF THE EARLY 1930S

The Great Depression proved disastrous for commercial banks. In an environment of falling incomes and widespread unemployment, defaults

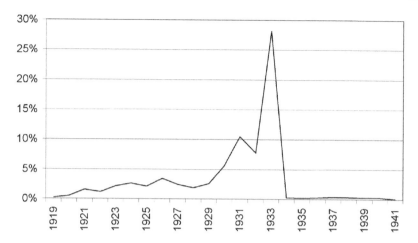

Figure 4. Failure of Federal Reserve Member Commercial Banks as a Percentage of Total Federal Reserve Member Commercial Banks, 1919–1941.

Source: Banking Studies.

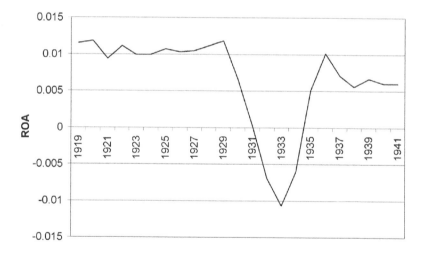

Figure 5. Return on Assets of Federal Reserve Member Banks, 1919–1941.

Source: Banking and Monetary Statistics.

on loans, together with the devaluation of the collateral backing those loans, contributed to an acute crisis in commercial banking. A downward spiral was generated as the loss of depositor confidence in bank solvency provoked bank runs, which in turn produced bank failures and further undermined depositor confidence (see Figure 4). State and nation-ally-chartered commercial banks in operation dropped from 24,258 in 1929 to 15,021 by 1934. These disastrous circumstances culminated in an acute profitability crisis for commercial banks. While the return on assets hovered between 0.99 percent and 1.19 percent throughout the 1920s, it had dipped to -1.07 percent by 1933 (see Figure 5).[21]

The crisis in commercial banking ramified throughout the economy. As bank failures destroyed deposits,[22] this put downward pressure on the money supply, thereby intensifying the economic downturn. In addition, the instability of the commercial banking sector compromised transactions in the economy, which further undermined confidence in the banking system. This process reduced the decline of the deposit base of commercial banks until the passage of the New Deal banking reforms in 1933 (Figure 6). In the midst of this cascading crisis, surviving commercial banks increasingly began to hold excess reserves as protection against bank runs.[23] Friedman and Schwartz indicate that even though the Federal Reserve increased the high-powered money available in the banking system, the increased hold-ings of excess reserves, in combination with withdrawals, devastated the money supply.[24]

As this situation spiraled downward, the use of expansionary mon-etary policy was thwarted in part because of the perverse implications of this crisis in commercial bank profitability. Before the Banking Act

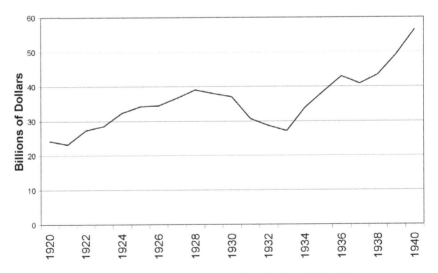

Figure 6. Bank Deposits, Federal Reserve Member Banks, 1920–1941.

Source: Banking and Monetary Statistics.

of 1933, commercial banks paid interest on demand deposits. This represented a serious burden to commercial banks, which were facing both substantial loan losses and dismal prospects for earnings on their loan portfolios. In response to this dilemma, and to enhance their liquidity in the event of banking panics, banks had increasingly shifted into holding short-term government securities. By 1932, "investments" (mostly in government securities) comprised 50 percent of bank earning portfolios among members of the Federal Reserve System (Epstein and Ferguson 1984, 969). This situation created an important obstacle to expansionary monetary policy. Epstein and Ferguson argue that the Federal Reserve briefly experimented with open market operations to increase the money supply, but the unintended result of this policy was to further squeeze bank profits by diminishing banks' earnings on their government securities.[25] Alarmed by this additional drag on their profitability, commercial banks succeeded in pressuring the Federal Reserve to abandon expansionary monetary policy. Epstein and Ferguson contend that Keynes was aware of the desperate reliance of commercial banks on their earnings from government securities and its perverse implications for monetary policy. They claim that it is for this reason that Keynes declared that "(. . .) in the United States the fear of the [Federal Reserve System] Member Banks lest they should be unable to cover their expenses is an obstacle to the adoption of a wholehearted cheap money policy"(in Epstein and Ferguson 1984, 957).[26]

As the downward spiral of bank failures and contraction of the money supply gained momentum, this further drained the economy of bank credit. Under such disastrous banking conditions, even otherwise creditworthy borrowers found refinancing increasingly unavailable. As Adolph Berle, member of the New Deal Brains Trust later recounted:

> The greatest single need [in 1933], it seemed to me, was to undergird the credit of the perfectly legitimate operations which were the basis of the (. . .) economy, when practically every one of them was facing default, sometimes because they couldn't pay their charges but more often because their debts were falling due and there was no place they could refinance them. And that was as true of the little farmer in Iowa as it was of the big railroad systems. So essentially the idea was to under gird the credit and simultaneously to get some spending power into the population (. . .) in Olson 1988, 87–88.

By early 1933, the commercial banking system was undeniably in profound disarray. Runs on commercial banks reached such disasterous proportions that it has been estimated that close to 10 percent of the nation's deposits were being withdrawn per week (Klebaner 1974, 133). The situation threatened to implode when the states of New York and Illinois suspended banking operations on the eve of Roosevelt's inauguration on Saturday March 4, 1933. In anticipation of the effect that this announcement would have on commercial banking nationwide, Roosevelt declared a national bank holiday on March 5, set to last until March 9 (it was later extended through March 13). Faced with this virtual cessation of financial intermediation, banking reform loomed as an urgent priority for the incoming Roosevelt administration.

THE EMERGING CRITIQUE OF DIVERSIFIED FINANCIAL CAPITALIST FIRMS IN THE EARLY 1930s

In the midst of the widespread suffering of the Great Depression and the seemingly bottomless crisis of the commercial banking system, public antipathy toward finance accelerated. Perhaps the most often cited indication of the extent to which finance had fallen into disrepute is Roosevelt's public condemnation of finance. His inaugural address stated that the unscrupulous money changers" now stood "indicted in the court of public opinion, rejected by the hearts and minds of men":

> Stripped of the lure of profit by which to induce our people to follow their false leadership, they have resorted to exhortations, pleading tearfully for restored confidence. They know only the rules of a generation of self-seekers. They have no vision, and when there is no vision the people perish.
>
> The money changers have fled from their high seats in the temple of our civilization. We may now restore that temple to the ancient truths. The measure of the restoration lies in the extent to which we apply social values more noble than mere monetary profit.[27]

Roosevelt explicitly linked the banking crisis to excessive speculation by bankers in his "fireside chat" of March 12, 1933:

> We had a bad banking situation. Some of our bankers had shown themselves either incompetent or dishonest in their handling of the people's funds. They had used the money entrusted to them in speculations and unwise loans. This was, of course, not true in the vast majority of our banks, but it was true in enough of them to shock the people for a time into a sense of insecurity and to put them into a frame of mind

where they did not differentiate, but seemed to assume that the acts of a comparative few had tainted them all. It was the government's job to straighten out this situation and do it as quickly as possible (in Krooss 1969, 2711).

As the Great Depression persisted and successive waves of bank failures continued, public debate flourished about the reasons for the turmoil and the appropriate remedies to prevent the recurrence of such calamities in the future. The Pecora-Gray hearings (1932–1934) publicized many notorious activities alleged to have occurred in diversified financial capitalist firms, and thereby played an influential role in promoting the public perception that diversified financial capitalist firms were inclined to speculative excess (as well as conflicts of interest). One of the most sensational early banking failures, the Bank of the United States in December 1930, was attributed to nefarious activities which were largely carried on through the bank's securities affiliates (Perkins 1971, 496–7).[28] Even the largest and most prestigious financial enterprises were subject to public condemnation. For example, National City Bank (the world's second largest bank at the time and predecessor of today's Citigroup) and its securities affiliate, National City Company (the US largest investment bank in the late 1920s), stood publicly accused of all sorts of dubious and possibly illegal practices stemming from their diversified financial capitalist activities.[29] At the conclusion of the hearings, one famous columnist of the period declared that "[t]he only thing that some of our great financial institutions overlooked during the years of boom was the installation of a roulette-wheel for the convenience of depositors" (in Carosso 1970, 330).

One important aspect of the case against diversified financial capitalist firms was the argument that the linkages between commercial and investment banking encouraged commercial banks to extend credit for speculative purposes. The growing tendency of Federal Reserve member banks to make loans on securities at the same time that they were becoming more involved with investment banking may be regarded as evidence of this propensity (see Figure 7). When the stock market crashed, many of these loans were highly compromised, particularly in situations in which corporate securities themselves had been presented as collateral for the initial loans.[30] To the degree that commercial bank loan portfolios were dependant on the performance of stock markets, instability in securities markets was transmitted to the commercial banking system.

While many factors arguably contributed to commercial banks' allocation of credit towards activities associated with securities markets (particularly in the context of a booming stock market), public policy responses

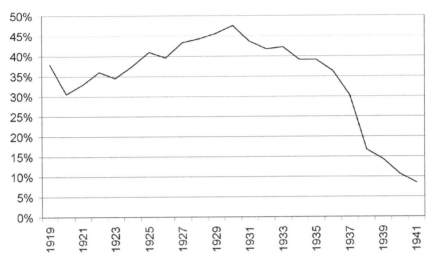

Figure 7. Commercial Bank Loans Made on Securities as a Percentage of Total Commercial Bank Loans, 1919–1941.

Source: Banking and Monetary Statistics.

focused on the organizational form of the diversified financial capitalist firm. Senator Carter Glass, a recognized authority in banking matters owing to his role in the creation of the Federal Reserve System, played a particularly prominent role in championing the abolition of diversified financial capitalist firms as a central component of the reform of American finance. For some time, Glass had argued that the relationship between commercial banks and their investment banking affiliates had contaminated the banking system with "stock gamblers," and he saw the separation of commercial and investment banking as necessary to preserve the integrity of the banking system (Glass 1929). Indeed, Glass succeeded in having the divorce of commercial and investment banking incorporated in the 1932 democratic platform.

The case built against the blending of commercial and investment banking parallels many of the critiques of diversified financial capitalist firms presented in Chapter 3. The extensive study co-authored by Glass' confidante Parker Willis depicts a slippery slope in which the investment banking arms of commercial banks created increasing pressure to intertwine commercial bank loan portfolios with the fortunes of securities markets during the 1920s:

> From such activities [underwriting stocks and bonds] [investment banking affiliates] had then passed to stock market operations, including the purchase or "accumulation" of stocks in the market which seemed

to be low in price, or were susceptible of being advanced in price by manipulation. Thus, working with the funds of the parent organizations, they had become intermediaries through which the savings of the public (. . .) were siphoned off into the stock market, there to furnish the basis of operations intended for the speculative profit of those who had engineered them (Willis 1934a, 67).

Ultimately, Willis concludes that the blending of commercial and investment banking was an ill-advised experiment in American finance:

> Accordingly, the tendency of investment banking to develop as a parasitic growth, drawing its support from commercial banking and constituting a diversion of the funds of the latter, notwithstanding that they were normally called-for as a means of liquidating demand obligations, presented numerous elements of danger, which did not, however, secure recognition at an early date. As often happens in financial development, it was an incidental phase of investment banking which originally operated to bring to the front the hazards that were involved in the maintenance of commercial and investment banking as phases of the activity of the same institution (Willis 1934b, 178).[31]

One particular critique of diversified financial capitalist firms merits additional consideration. Glass was also concerned that the provision of credit for speculative purposes had become detrimental to the provision of credit for use as investment capital. As an advocate of the "real bills" doctrine, Glass also wanted to ensure that banks were intermediating savings to provide investment capital to fulfill the "legitimate needs of business" (Perkins 1971, 499).[32] Instead, conditions had been created that promoted the "misapplication of credit" (Willis 1934a, 53). To the extent that banks with investment banking affiliates were inclined to allocate credit towards speculative activities rather than financing investment by productive capitalist firms, this "misapplication of credit" funneled the economy's savings away from the provision of investment capital.

Diversified financial capitalist firms, tainted by their association with the reviled money-trusts, became emblematic of the abuses of financiers. Under these circumstances, it was politically feasible to act on this growing critique of finance to implement an ambitious program of banking reforms. The New Deal could bring together a heterogeneous group to support their banking reforms in part because of their common desire to reap political advantage by championing the growing public animosity towards financiers. The anti-finance sentiment of the early 1930s created opportunities for the Roosevelt administration to intervene in the re-organization of the financial sector in ways that might have been considered far too radical in the absence of public animosity towards finance. And finance largely acquiesced to these reforms, possibly because they feared other alternatives that it found even less appealing. Rumors of nationalization circulated prior to the Banking Act of 1933, and such rumors were occasionally inflamed by comments such as those of Albert Agnew, General Counsel for the Federal Reserve Bank of San Francisco, who warned ominously from the pages of a banking periodical: "Either the bankers of this country will realize that they are guardians of the moneys committed to their charge, and will conduct themselves accordingly, or banking will cease to be a private enterprise and will become a purely government function" (in Burns 1974, 73).

"FINANCE-AS-SERVANT" AND THE CRITIQUE OF THE DIVERSIFIED FINANCIAL CAPITALIST FIRM

For many decades following the New Deal banking reforms, it was widely accepted that blending commercial and investment banking had deleterious effects on bank stability and promoted speculation during the 1920s.[33] As late as 1986, former chairman of the Federal Reserve Board of Governors Paul Volcker reinforced the widely shared consensus that:

> Congressional hearings on the securities practices of banks disclosed that bank affiliates had underwritten and sold unsound and speculative securities, published deliberately misleading prospectuses, manipulated the price of particular securities, misappropriated corporate opportunities to bank officers, engaged in insider lending practices and unsound transactions with affiliates. Evidence also pointed to cases where banks had made unsound loans to assist their affiliates and to protect the securities underwritten by the affiliates. Confusion by the public as to whether they were dealing with a bank or its securities affiliate and loss of confidence in the banking system were also cited as adverse consequences of the securities affiliate system (in Benston 1990, 12).[34]

However, as the Glass-Steagall Act came under attack in the late 1980s and 1990s, the prevailing interpretation of the justification for Glass-Steagall was subjected to renewed critique. Benston (1990) provides a valuable catalogue of the scholarship refuting the case for Glass-Steagall.[35] In general, this literature is concerned with evaluating whether the blending of commercial and investment banking can be demonstrated to have contributed to abuses in securities markets, bank instability, and other problems cited at the time as the justifications for Glass-Steagall.[36] As this literature gained prominence and the rejection of Glass-Steagall gathered momentum, the conventional wisdom was inverted. Where previously it had been acceptable to assert the unquestionable necessity of Glass-Steagall, by the 1990s it became acceptable to assert its unmitigated folly. Glass-Steagall was increasingly characterized as a regulatory framework based on little more than misplaced vengeance[37] supported by no factual basis whatsoever: "three different sets of congressional hearings held over four years during the 1930s, none of the accusations of conflicts of interest, improper banking activities, or excessive risk attached to banks' securities activities was proved" (England, undated).

While we have presented above some of the prominent arguments concerning the blending of commercial and investment banking that circulated in the early 1930s, no effort is made here to evaluate these critiques empirically. Our ultimate purpose is to evaluate the extent to which New Deal banking reforms were congruent with the subsequent development of Keynesian welfare state capitalism, and our primary focus is the exploration of the "finance-as-servant" proposition and the question of how New Deal financial reforms may have affected the relative bargaining power of financial and productive capitalist firms. Hence we leave aside the assessment of whether or not New Deal reforms were an appropriate response to the evidence available at the time (or evidence subsequently available) concerning bank stability, speculation or other matters. It is conceivable that New Deal reforms may be deemed an unjustifiable response to the conditions of the early 1930s, yet this financial regulatory structure might still be of great benefit to Keynesian welfare state capitalism. Conversely, New Deal reforms might have been entirely appropriate in the context of the early 1930s, yet they could arguably have been inimical to the era of Keynesian welfare state following World War II.

A variety of charges were levelled against the blending of commercial and investment banking are related to the "finance-as-servant" thematic developed in previous chapters. If the commercial banking arm of this type of diversified financial capitalist firm is oriented to allocating credit to support transactions in securities markets rather than providing investment capital to productive capitalist firms, this may be deleterious to a pro-investment agenda. And since the stability of the banking system is a necessary condition of pro-investment economic reforms, the separation of commercial and investment banking is supportive of Keynesian welfare state capitalism insofar as it deters the speculative activities that may jeopardize bank stability. However we refrain from evaluating whether the Glass-Steagall Act was justified to prevent a recurrence of either the speculation of the 1920s and/or bank instability in the 1930s. Instead our focus concerns the question of the bargaining power of diversified financial capitalist firms vis-à-vis productive capitalist firms seeking infusions of investment capital.

In terms of our analysis of bargaining power, diversified financial capitalist firms—or "department store" banks as the business press of the day called them (Carosso 1970, 276)[38]—have the potential to reshape competitive conditions among suppliers of investment capital. Diversified financial capitalist firms do not wish productive capitalist firms to benefit from competition between commercial and investment banks as providers of investment capital, as this puts downward pressure on the profits of both their commercial bank and investment banking arms. If diversified financial capitalist firms have sufficient market power in both commercial and investment banking, they may be able to bid up the costs of accessing investment capital in its various forms. Thus diversified financial capitalist firms enhance the possibility that financial capital may gain the bargaining power relative to productive capital.[39]

No claim is made that the analyses of the day explicitly engaged with the question of the relative bargaining power of productive capitalist firms and financial capitalist firms as they negotiate access to investment capital. Given the prevailing conditions in the Great Depression, those seeking to promote economic recovery via investment realized that little bank credit would be forthcoming—on any terms—if the commercial banking system was left in such disarray. Under such circumstances, it was not likely that the architects of New Deal banking reforms were looking forward to anticipate the financial regulatory landscape amenable to Keynesian welfare state capitalism—particularly given that the theoretical underpinnings for the Keynesian welfare state were still in the process of being elaborated by Keynes. But whether by accident or by design, the abolishing of diversified financial capitalist firms reconfigured competitive conditions among financial capitalist firms, such that productive capitalist firms seeking funds could benefit from competition between providers of investment capital. And whether this outcome was intentional or unintentional, this regulatory framework prevailed throughout the golden age of Keynesian welfare state capitalism.

Chapter Five

The Contradictory Imperatives of New Deal Banking Reforms

"FINANCE-AS-SERVANT" AND THE CONTRADICTORY IMPERATIVES OF NEW DEAL BANKING REFORMS

Having narrowly averted the collapse of US banking in March of 1933, New Dealers recognized that further economic reforms would be thwarted by continued crisis in the banking system. In response to this crisis, the Roosevelt administration quickly passed the Banking Act of June 16, 1933.[1] We focus on the Banking Act of 1933 (and one subsequent provision in the Banking Act of 1935) as the regulatory framework intended to both stabilize the commercial banking system and enable it to play a supportive role for the greater project of economic recovery. This chapter will survey some highlights of this New Deal banking reform, namely interest rate controls and the introduction of deposit insurance implemented by the Banking Act of 1933, as well as the limitations on entry into commercial banking contained in the Banking Act of 1935. However our major focus is the separation of commercial and investment banking, known in common parlance as the Glass-Steagall Act, despite the fact that Glass-Steagall is not an Act *per se* but several subsections of the Banking Act of 1933.[2]

The preamble of the Banking Act of 1933 indicates that it is "[a]n act to provide for the safer and more effective use of the assets of banks, to regulate interbank control, to prevent the undue diversion of funds into speculative operations, and for other purposes" (in Kross, 1969, 2758). Given that stability in the banking system was a prerequisite to the success of any further pro-investment economic reforms, many of its provisions, such as deposit insurance, sought to stabilize the commercial banking system. The Glass-Steagall separation of commercial and investment banking can also be understood as a measure intended to promote stability in the banking system. In response to the critique of the pro-speculative propensities of diversified financial capitalist firms discussed in Chapter 4, the Act sought to diminish the conflicts of interest—and other incentives that encourage speculation—that may emerge when commercial and investment banking become organizationally entwined. By shielding commercial banks from these speculative pressures, Glass-Steagall sought to prevent the deposit base of the economy from being excessively channeled towards speculative purposes. This deterrence of commercial bank involvement in speculative activity was understood as enhancing the stability of the commercial banking system, and it responded to Senator Glass' concerns that the "misapplication" of credit for speculative purposes deprives "legitimate business" of funds (see Chapter 4).

While questions of speculative pressures within banking and their influence on the uses of credit and bank stability were foremost in the explicit rationale for the Banking Act, this chapter argues that there was a further dimension of the Glass-Steagall Act that had important ramifications for subsequent pro-investment economic reforms. We argue that Glass-Steagall constituted a financial regulatory framework that enhanced the bargaining power of productive capitalist firms relative to financial capitalist firms. This constraint on the bargaining power of financial capitalist firms was supportive of a longer-term pro-investment agenda insofar as it created conditions conducive to downward pressure on the price of investment capital. Thus alongside the creation of a regulatory framework that sought to stabilize the commercial banking system, New Deal banking reforms were also conducive to the provision of investment capital on terms that were supportive of investment spending.

However, the New Deal financial regulatory framework (consciously or unconsciously) confronted a complex regulatory puzzle that is discernible via the "finance-as-servant" analysis developed in previous chapters. If finance is to "serve" a pro-investment agenda by extending investment capital on favorable terms, this might be deleterious to the profitability of financial intermediaries, including commercial banks.[3] This is a perilous situation, given that unprofitable banks can potentially threaten the stability of the commercial banking system. Thus any financial reform that supports downward pressure on the price of investment capital by diminishing the bargaining power of financial capitalist firms implies a possible (although not necessary) downward pressure on commercial bank profitability. To the extent that this downward pressure on bank profitability occurs, this conflicts with the necessity of supporting profitability in the commercial banking system. At the same time, efforts to support the profitability of commercial banks must avoid any measure that might exert upward pressure on the costs of accessing funds, for this is inimical to a pro-investment agenda.

This chapter re-considers the New Deal banking reforms in the light of the multiple and potentially conflicting imperatives visible in this "finance-as-servant" dilemma. The Banking Acts were obliged to enhance commercial bank profitability (to safeguard the stability of the commercial banking system) and constrain it (insofar as promoting the availability of cheap investment capital may undermine bank profitability). This chapter presents the case that the Glass-Steagall Act, in combination with several other provisions included in the Banking Acts of 1933 and 1935, can be viewed as an attempt to manage these potentially divergent imperatives emanating from the "finance-as-servant" agenda.

Glass-Steagall set the stage for a domestic financial framework that prevailed throughout the epoch of Keynesian welfare state capitalism. American finance became characterized by "financial compartmentalization," in which all financial capitalist firms—commercial banks, investment banks, savings and loans, pension funds, insurance companies, and so forth—were placed in separate regulatory categories and prevented from crossing these regulatory boundaries. This domestic financial regulatory framework presided over the post-war *"pax financus,"* a period of relative financial stability combined with low real interest rates that prevailed during the golden age of Keynesian welfare state capitalism in the United States. But while in some respects this New Deal financial regulatory framework did an admirable job of managing the potentially divergent imperatives implied by the "finance-as-servant" agenda, Chapter 6 will ague that it nonetheless set in motion tensions that ultimately undermined this organization of financial intermediation. Financial compartmentalization began to fray as the Keynesian welfare state began its decline, and ultimately Glass-Steagall was repealed in 1999.

The argument presented in this chapter begins with an examination of the aspects of the New Deal banking reforms that supported the profitability of commercial banks. Secondly, we present the case that the Glass-Steagall provisions separating commercial and investment banking were supportive of the bargaining power of productive capitalist firms relative to financial capitalist firms, and that this situation was conducive to the accessibility of investment capital on advantageous terms. The chapter concludes by considering the ramifications of these regulatory provisions on competitive conditions in the financial sector. Via its navigation of the contradictory imperatives of this "finance-as-servant" agenda, the New Deal banking reforms reshaped competitive conditions both between commercial banks and among all other financial intermediaries. While it is frequently asserted that New Deal banking regulations were unambiguously anti-competitive[4], the analysis that emanates from the "finance-as-servant" perspective implies that competition was reshaped in contradictory ways. In some respects, these reforms intensified competition among financial intermediaries, while in other respects they constrained it. Chapter 6 will argue that the contradictory implications for competition set in motion forces that ultimately undermined this New Deal regulatory structure.

New Deal Banking Reforms and Commercial Bank Profitability

Chapter 4 discussed bank profitability as a necessary condition for the stability of the commercial banking system. Since the profitability of the commercial banks that survived the waves of bank failures was still unsustainably dismal (see Figure 5, Chapter 4), bank profitability was an important consideration in framing the New Deal banking reforms. Ironically, the importance of supporting bank profitability was made more acute given that the Glass-Steagall Act was to put further constraints on the avenues through which commercial banks might attempt to enhance their profitability. The separation of commercial and investment banking largely foreclosed the possiblity that banks might supplement their profitability by non-banking financial capitalist activities. Thus Glass-Steagall forced banks to rely on taking deposits and making loans at a time when this line of business was in crisis. Bankers warned of the ominous burden this imposed upon them during the 1932 Senate debates concerning the separation of commercial and investment banking:

> Fifteen years ago 90 per cent of the business of the bank of which I am president was commercial business and 90 per cent of our income came from those accounts. We have always been a commercial bank. We are not a Wall Street bank and never have been a Wall Street bank. The trend of business in the last 12 or 15 years has been commercial business, down, down, down, and last year [1931] only 22 per cent of our income came from the commercial business; 28 per cent of our income came from loans on securities, bond and stocks—I do not mean speculative loans; 21 per cent came from investments, municipal, State bonds, and things like that; 49 per cent of our revenue came from a class of income that is going to be largely prohibited under this act" (in Peach 1941, 25).[5]

Because of both the dismal profitability of banks in the early 1930s and the further constraints put on commercial banking,[6] New Deal banking regulations were obliged to incorporate some supports to bank profitability. But while restoring the profitability of commercial banking was urgent, the authors of New Deal banking regulations could not enhance the profitability of the banking system with measures that would jeopardize the larger agenda for economic recovery by putting upward pressure on the costs of accessing investment capital. To consider how this dilemma might be navigated, we return to our earlier analysis of commercial bank profitability. Chapter 3 discussed commercial bank profitability in terms of the "spread" between the interest rate paid to secure deposits versus the interest rate received on loans. Since New Dealers would be loath to increase the latter, their efforts to support the profitability of commercial banks focused on lowering the former. If banks are able to access funds more cheaply in the first phase of financial intermediation, and/or if they have access to more funds, this enhances their potential profitability. This chapter contends that New Deal banking reforms supported commercial bank profitability by putting downward pressure on banks' costs of accessing funds, while increasing the volume of funds intermediated by banks. In particular, we examine the proposition that deposit insurance, interest rate controls on deposits, and the end of free banking functioned synergistically to support bank profitability in this manner.

To end the paralyzing waves of bank failures in the commercial banking system, Congressman Henry Steagall lead the campaign to include a national system of deposit insurance in the Banking Act of 1933. The Federal Deposit Insurance Corporation (FDIC) was established to insure deposits (up to some maximum amount) in the event of bank failure. While the initial funds for the FDIC were provided by the United States Treasury and the twelve Federal Reserve Banks, ongoing funding of the Deposit Insurance Fund was intended to be financed by the premiums paid by commercial banks. Despite their initial opposition,[7] commercial bankers were quickly convinced of the merits of deposit insurance. A traumatized public evidently placed considerable value on a government supported guarantee of the security of their savings held in deposits. Thus the introduction of deposit insurance reversed the precipitous decline in deposits that had devastated the banking system prior to the passage of the Banking Act of 1933. Deposits recovered from their low point of $27 billion in 1933 to surpass $49 billion by 1939 in nominal terms (see Figure 6, Chapter 4)—an impressive feat in light of the deflationary context of the 1930s. Moreover, the introduction of deposit insurance stemmed the flood of bank failures. Despite a modest spike in the late 1930s, the relatively modest rates of bank failures in the decades following the creation of deposit insurance contrast sharply with the high rates of bank failures that had characterized American banking prior to the advent of the FDIC (see Figure 8). Not until the 1980s, when the New Deal regulatory framework for banking was rapidly dissolving, did bank failures surge above this relatively low level.

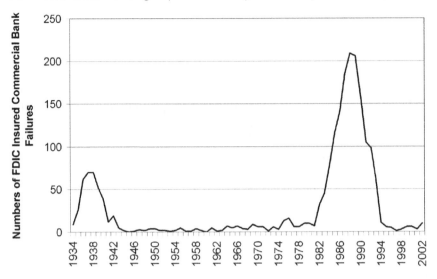

Figure 8. Numbers of FDIC-Member Commercial Bank Failures, 1934–2002.

Source: *Historical Statistics on Banking.*

Alongside deposit insurance, the Banking Act of 1933 placed interest rate controls on both savings and checking deposits. Regulation Q set maximum interest rates that could be paid on savings deposits.[8] The Banking Act of 1933 also forbade the previously common practice of paying interest on checking accounts. In public debate at the time of the Banking Act's passage, these interest rate controls were described as a measure that would protect banks from having to resort to more speculative activities. It was claimed that excessive competition over access to deposits had been responsible for bidding up the costs of attracting funds for commercial banks, and that the high costs of securing loanable funds in turn encouraged banks to migrate towards riskier lending practices connected with securities markets in order to earn sufficient returns to cover the costs of securing funds (see Friedman and Schwartz 1963, 443).[9] By controlling the cost of securing deposits, Senator Glass argued that interest rate controls on deposits would "put a stop to the competition between banks in payment of interest, which frequently induce[s] banks to pay excessive interest on time deposits and has many times over again brought banks into serious trouble"(in Hayes 1987, 20).

Whatever the merits of the argument linking interest rate controls on deposits and the deterrence of speculation, interest rate controls are supportive of commercial bank profitability in the sense that they reduce expenses.[10] Depositors—such as firms that require checking privileges in order to manage payrolls and accounts receivable and payable—were compelled to provide funds to banks interest-free. (Ironically, this represents a situation in which capitalist firms who required checking accounts "served" commercial banks.) Regulation Q also moderated the expense of attracting savings deposits in those periods in which the prevailing interest rates on savings deposits were above below the Regulation Q cap. Interest rate controls appear to have had a salutary impact on commercial bank profitability in the context of the 1930s. Commercial banks paid as much as 2 cents of interest for every dollar in deposits prior to 1929, while by the late 1930s they paid under one half of one cent of interest per dollar of deposits (see Figure 9).[11]

Deposit insurance and interest rate controls worked together to support commercial bank profitability. The interest income forgone by depositors under the regime of New Deal interest rate controls represents an implicit subsidy to commercial banks. Government-orchestrated deposit insurance made possible a situation in which depositors were willing to provide this subsidy to commercial banks in exchange for the security conferred by deposit insurance. The synergistic effects of both deposit insurance and interest rate controls supported commercial bank profitability both because of the greater availability of funds and because of diminished cost of securing each dollar of deposits. Remarkably, while deposits grew 81 percent by the end of the 1930s from their low point in 1933, the total interest paid by commercial banks on deposits declined dramatically (see Figure 10).

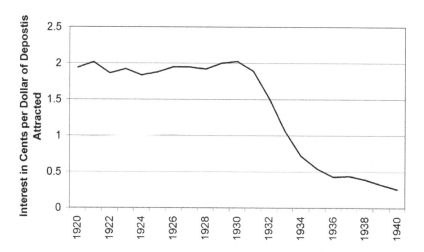

Figure 9. Interest Paid on Deposits per Dollar of Deposits. Attracted at Feeral Reserve Member Banks, 1920–1940.

Source: *Banking and Monetary Statistics.*

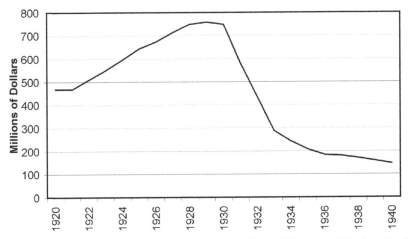

Figure 10. Total Interest Paid on Deposits at Federal Reserve Member Banks, 1920–1940.

Source: *Banking and Monetary Statistics.*

However, the introduction of deposit insurance further complicates the state's relationship with commercial banks. The moral hazard issues discussed previously in the context of the lender of last resort function of the central bank are now compounded by the fact that deposit insurance extends the government-backed safety net to depositors. Since depositors are reassured that their deposits are protected in the event of a bank failure, they are less likely to instigate a bank run if they perceive that their bank is engaging in activities that may provoke the banks' failure. Since the disciplinary vigilance of depositors is relaxed, banks may be emboldened to engage in riskier activities that would be viewed as imprudent in the absence of deposit insurance. Meanwhile, the state faces new difficulties. If a bank crisis of sufficiently large magnitude overwhelms the resources of the Deposit Insurance Fund, it is plausible to expect the government to come to the aid of the Deposit Insurance Fund. This large potential liability provides the state with an additional incentive to safeguard the profitability of commercial banks. Insofar as profitable banks are more resilient during turbulent banking conditions, profitability within the commercial banking sector is protective of the Deposit Insurance Fund. Thus with the introduction of deposit insurance, the FDIC emerged as a governmental body with a deep concern for the general profitability of commercial banking. This concern for commercial bank profitability was particularly acute in the days following the banking crises of the early 1930s, as a recent FDIC review of the history of deposit insurance has summarized:

For its part, the FDIC was faced with a dilemma [during 1934]. Although the bank failure rate had dropped precipitously, and the capital rehabilitation program of the RFC [Reconstruction Finance Corporation] and the FDIC had been modestly successful, the banking system was not strong and the prospects for bank earnings were not bright. Additionally, the fears and uncertainties regarding bank failures had not been dispelled by 1934 and indeed would not recede for more than two decades. The FDIC was thus faced with the problems of protecting the earnings of insured banks until capital and reserve positions could be rebuilt, while conserving what was by historical standards a modest deposit insurance fund (FDIC 1998, 36).

As the Great Depression continued, the problem of over-banking persisted as a subject of debate among banking regulators. The ban on interstate banking continued to contribute to the large number of commercial banks in the US banking system, as did the failure of Senator Glass' efforts to allow state-wide branching by national banks. Hostility to branching was championed by small banks, who argued that the "money trusts" would destroy competition and drain savings into the large financial centers.[12] As Brain Trust member Adolph Berle indicated in his speech to the New York State Bankers Association following the passage of the Act, political sensitivities and particularly the prevailing antipathy towards large banks was sufficient to make the widespread adoption of national branch banking politically unattainable:

> You could probably get some of the desired security by a chain banking system. But rightly or wrongly, the outlying parts of the country are firm in their distrust of the methods of finance of the great centers, notably New York, Philadelphia, Boston, [and] Chicago. Whether this is justifiable, only the outcome can tell, but to date, the results of eastern domination have not been too good. It does not answer to say to such districts that the great units in New York, let us say, have been safe and liquid, if the West is able to demonstrate that the result of that liquidity has been to crucify the rest of the country. You have, therefore, a very real situation, and the fact that it manifested itself (sic) politically in a direction which we may believe and do believe was probably unsound, does not remove the problem. Opposition to chain banking is still so great that we shall not have it (. . .). We have, therefore, the great refuge that has been supplied in England, Canada, and Australia left on one side (1933, 10).

Under these circumstances, the principle of "free banking" came under attack. Banking authorities did not wish to encourage the entry of dubious banks that would be prone to failure, thus imposing upon the Deposit Insurance Fund and potentially igniting destabilizing contagion effects within the banking system. But an increase in the numbers of banks in general could pose problems for the New Deal banking reforms intended to support commercial bank profitability. As commercial banks returned to profitabilty under the New Deal regulatory framework, this could trigger new entry into commercial banking, thereby potentially re-igniting competition for deposits and creating pressure to subvert interest rates controls. If banks did find such ways to compete for deposits, this could put upward pressure on their costs and thus diminish their profitability. Thus New Dealers feared a return to "overbanking" that was a continual possiblity so long as free banking persisted. Berle illustrated this dilemma as follows:

> Is there any sense in having the First Trust Company on one side of the street competing with the Second State Bank on the other to draw deposits from one unit to make its own unit larger?
>
> There can be only one result. The net pool is not enlarged. That can be done only by credit or by the slow growth of population and the growth of production, in the particular community which you serve. Competition between the two banks can only end in weakening one at the expense of the other, to the advantage of neither (1933, 8).

The FDIC became an important source of pressure to eliminate "unfettered" competition among banks, and instead sought to create conditions of "rightful competition" in commercial banking (FDIC, 1998, 33). This culminated in the elimination of free banking in the Banking Act of 1935. The Act gave chartering bodies a degree of discretion over entry into commercial banking, and one of the criteria that had to be met before a new commercial bank could be chartered included regulatory consideration of the "future earnings prospects" of the bank.[13] This obligation stood as an explicit official acknowledgement that the profitability of commercial banks was a consideration that should guide banking regulators. Pleased with the restraints to competition implied by the Act, the FDIC hailed the 1935 Act as an aid to "prevent the recurrence of the evil which is to be greatly feared (. . .) the return of the over-banked condition of the twenties" (in Klebaner 1990, 162).

As a result of the bank failures of the 1920s and the crisis afflicting commercial banking in the 1930s, the numbers of commercial banks in operation in the United States was dramatically reduced. At its highpoint in 1921, there had been 29,417 state and nationally chartered commercial banks in the United States, and by 1929, this figure stood at 24,258

(Members of the Staff of the Board of Governors of the Federal Reserve System, 1941, 419). The bank failures of the 1930s, together with the new restrictiveness in permitting entry into commercial banking following the passage of the Banking Act of 1935, reduced the number of FDIC-insured commercial banks in operation to 13,538 by 1939. Klebaner claims that by 1940, the average population per commercial bank had risen to 7,400 nearly double the ratio of 1920 (Klebaner 1974, 158). Moreover, the more restrictive regulatory posture on commercial bank entry ensured that any improvement in banking conditions did not provoke a wave of new entrants. Klebaner cites an unnamed report of the Controller of the Currency claiming that 1936 marked a quarter-century swing to "the extreme of unduly restricted approval" of new bank charters (1974, 158). Until the late 1980s, the number of commercial banks remained stable (see Figure 11).

Following the passage of the Banking Act of 1933, commercial bank profitability recovered from the disastrous levels of the previous years (see Figure 12). This is not to say that this regulatory framework was a panacea for commercial banking, for the difficult conditions of the Great Depression created challenges in banking throughout the 1930s. Just as we do not claim that the New Deal banking reforms solved the problems of commercial banking in the 1930s, we do not credit this regulatory framework with unilaterally causing the relative stability in banking throughout the

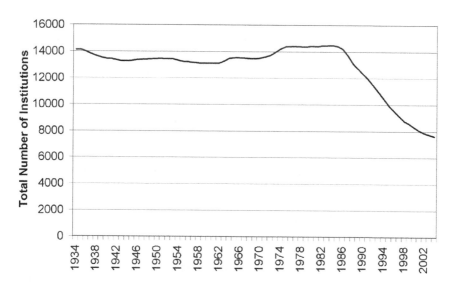

Figure 11. Number of FDIC-Insured Commercial Banks, 1934–2004.

Source: *Historical Statistics on Banking.*

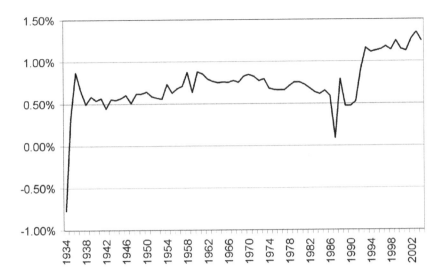

Figure 12. Return on Assets, FDIC-Member Commercial Banks, 1933–2002.

Sources: Federal Deposit Insurance Corporation Historical Statistics on Banking.

golden age of Keynesian welfare state capitalism. Both bank profitability and stability are shaped by many factors beyond those regulatory considerations discussed here. However, this regulatory framework did preside over a long period of relatively stable, profitable banking that coincided with Keynesian welfare state capitalism, and the regulatory framework succumbed to various pressures as the welfare state began its decline. While some elements of New Deal banking reforms (such as federal deposit insurance) continue until the present, Chapter 6 will describe how several of these reforms were dismantled as the Keynesian welfare state began to exhibit severe strain in the 1970s.

THE GLASS-STEAGALL AND FINANCE-AS-SERVANT

We have argued thus far that a project of economic reform seeking to ameliorate aggregate demand conditions will favor the provision investment capital on advantageous terms. But the New Deal banking reforms discussed thus far are not directly supportive of this goal. Deposit insurance, interest rate controls on deposits, and the end of free banking enhanced commercial bank profitability and thereby promoted the stability of the commercial banking system. While the stability of the commercial banking system was a necessary step towards the amelioration of aggregate demand conditions generally, it would have sabotaged aggregate demand conditions if banks were able to use their new advantages to exert upward pressure on the cost of accessing investment capital. To make the case that New Deal banking reforms were congruent with a pro-investment economic agenda, we return to our previous exploration of the concept of "finance-as-servant"to understand why these various measures were implemented alongside the Glass-Steagall Act.

The Banking Act of 1933 also included the Glass-Steagall subsections that prohibited the blending of commercial and investment banking. Section 20 of the Act required commercial banks belonging to the Federal Reserve System to divest themselves of their securities affiliates within one year.[14] In combination with a few other subsections of the Act,[15] this ended the combination of commercial and investment banking within a financial capitalist firm in the United States. (An exception was made to enable commercial banks to engage in the underwriting and dealing of certain government securities).[16] Following the passage of the Banking Act of 1933, American financial conglomerates were promptly dismantled.[17] The Glass-Steagall Act effectively ended the existence of the diversified financial capitalist firm that blended banking with other financial capitalist activities, and set the stage for the compartmentalization of finance that prevailed during the golden age of Keynesian welfare state capitalism. (In addition, Glass-Steagall, together with amendments to the Federal Reserve Act, also impeded the creation of diversified capitalist firms that blended financial capitalist activities, including banking, with productive capitalist or merchant capitalist activities.[18])

Our contention is that, under the particular historical and institutional circumstances of the American banking sector in the Great Depression, the Glass-Steagall prohibition on diversified financial capitalist firms was congruent with a pro-investment economic reform agenda. Given the various New Deal banking reforms that enhanced commercial bank profitability, Glass-Steagall created conditions that decreased the possibility that the supportive aspects of this regualtory framework would be exploited in order to exert upward pressure on the costs of securing investment capital. Instead, we argue that Glass-Steagall supported the bargaining power of productive capitalist firms relative to financial capitalist firms, and thus encouraged downward pressure on the costs of accessing investment capital. To illustrate this contention, we return briefly to the consideration of the "spread" between the costs of accessing funds and the income received by supplying funds. Our discussion now turns to the second phase of the intermediation process, namely the provision of funds by the financial intermediary to the end-user of the funds, and the relative bargaining positions of the productive capitalist firm seeking investment capital and the financial capitalist firms competing to provide it.

One factor that enhances the negotiating position of productive capitalist firms is vigorous competition among financial intermediaries as suppliers of investment capital. These competitive conditions among financial intermediaries are themselves shaped by a host of factors (including interstate or international limitations on the activities of financial capitalist firms, the demand for funds by entities other than productive capitalist firms, and so on). However, we will focus on the possible impacts of diversified financial capitalist firms on the competition among providers of investment capital.

Because it is able to engage in both commercial banking and investment banking, a diversified financial capitalist firm may be in an advantageous position to impede competition among providers of investment capital. It will certainly endeavor to prevent its own investment banking and commercial banking branches from engaging in such competition with each other. It can also cross-subsidize its activities or create other disincentives to deter productive capitalist firms from fulfilling their commercial banking needs and their investment banking needs with different financial capitalist firms. Moreover, productive capitalist firms may be reluctant to switch diversified financial capitalist firms if the existence of a previously established relationship mitigates informational difficulties. If diversified financial capitalist firms succeed in impeding the competition between commercial banks and investment banks, the range of options open to productive capitalist firms is narrowed and their bargaining power is reduced. The extent to which diversified financial capitalist firms may thwart competition among providers of investment capital at large is indeterminate (various factors must be taken into consideration including the number and size of diversified financial capitalist firms in the market). But even if conditions are not auspicious for diversified financial capitalist firms to effect such restraint on competition, advocates of pro-investment economic reform need to be mindful of the persistent threat that large diversified financial firms have the potential to disadvantage productive capitalist firms in their bargaining positions *vis-à-vis* the suppliers of investment capital, and thereby put upward pressure on the price of investment capital.

By prohibiting the blending of banking and non-banking financial capitalist activity within a single firm, Glass-Steagall limited the opportunity for financial capitalist firms to attenuate competition via the creation of diversified financial capitalist firms. Investment banks could continue to offer access to both debt and equity capital via securities markets. However, investment banks did not intermediate the bulk of domestic savings (thanks in large part to the distinctive privileges, such as deposit insurance, that were accorded solely to commercial banks). Commercial banks intermediated a large amount of domestic savings, yet they were excluded from offering access to investment capital via securities markets. Commercial banks could not supply equity capital, and their provision of debt capital was restricted to the vehicle of bank loans. Glass-Steagall, in combination with the other measures in the Banking Act discussed above, created a situation in which no financial capitalist firm could simultaneously dominate the supply of both debt and equity capital while accessing the bulk of the savings that resided in the deposit base.

Thus Glass-Steagall, together with the other New Deal banking reforms, can be understood as an attempt to navigate the contradictory imperatives confronting the architects of a financial regulatory framework intended to be supportive of a pro-investment economic reform agenda. New Deal banking reforms supported the profitability of commercial banks, but the Glass-Steagall provisions impeded commercial banks from using their distinctive privileges to dominate all financial capitalist activities and thereby potentially drive up the price of investment capital. Thus this regulatory framework enhanced the possibility that finance would "serve" the pro-investment agenda, while safeguarding the stability of that important servant, commercial banks. And to the extent that commercial banks were cushioned by the supports conveyed by this regulatory framework, they would be amenable to fulfil their intended role in the pro-investment agenda.

The New Deal financial regulatory framework served as the template for the financial compartmentalization that persisted throughout the golden age of Keynesian welfare state capitalism. Financial capitalist firms were classified according to the particular method through which they gather funds in the first moment of financial intermediation. Commercial banks had the exclusive ability to offer insured deposits while investment banks had the exclusive ability to underwrite securities. As this regulatory principle evolved further, insurance companies, pension funds, and other financial intermediaries were all separately regulated and confined to the gathering of savings in the manner characteristic of their particular regulatory classification. This regulatory framework had diverse impacts on competition in the first phase of financial intermediation. While all financial capitalist firms compete to attract savings, financial compartmentalization inhibited financial capitalist firms of different regulatory categories from competing with each other, in the sense that a financial capitalist firm of a given regulatory category could not access savings in the manner characteristic of other regulatory categories (commercial banks could not offer insurance or sell corporate securities, for example). However, competition for access to funds among financial capitalist firms within a given category could continue. This competition within a regulatory category varied according to a host of factors, including other regulatory provisions, such as the prohibition on interstate banking.

Meanwhile, in the market to provide investment capital to productive capitalist firms, competition could be vigorous insofar as investment banks and commercial banks could vie with each other (and increasingly over time, with other financial intermediaries such as pension funds and mutual funds). This competition in the second phase of financial intermediation helped to exert downward pressure on the cost of accessing investment capital. Thus deterrents to competition in the first phase of financial intermediation implied by financial compartmentalization did not necessarily moderate competition among financial capitalist firms as providers of investment capital. So long as competition was vigorous in the second phase of financial intermediation, New Deal banking reforms might enhance the profitability of commercial banks in the first phase of financial intermediation without necessarily subverting the agenda for the accessibility of investment capital on favorable terms in the second phase of financial intermediation. Thus New Deal banking reforms had ambiguous impacts on competition: they simultaneously encouraged competition among financial intermediaries in one respect while restraining it another respect.

The possibility that Glass-Steagall and its accompanying New Deal banking reforms responded to the imperatives animating the larger project of a pro-investment economic reform has been absent from the analyses of Glass-Steagall that flourished prior to its repeal in 1999. An important precursor to this literature was Friedman and Schwartz's influential *A Monetary History of the United States* (1963), which attributed banking failures during the depression to faulty government intervention rather than reproachable conduct on the part of financial capitalists. From this point of departure, numerous scholars sought to reinterpret New Deal financial regulation as a gratuitous and arbitrary impediment to the efficiency of financial markets. Thereafter, the justifications for Glass-Steagall that were advanced in the 1930s—particularly the question of whether the mixing of commercial and investment banking in the 1920s contributed to speculation and bank instability (see Chapter 4) have been laboriously refuted, leaving the impression that Glass-Steagall remained only as an artifact of an era in which public policy was contorted to indulge the politically expedient public condemnation of financiers. This condemnation of Glass-Steagall grew to be so vociferous that one might have wondered how a regulatory structure purported to lack virtually any redeeming merits (save perhaps the introduction of deposit insurance) could have persisted for over 60 years. Indeed, the name chosen for its successor legislation, the Financial Services Modernization Act (also known as the Gramm-Leach-Bliley Act) conveys the sense that the previous regulatory structure lacked the (apparently commendable) characteristics of modernity.

This analysis seeks neither to condemn nor celebrate the Glass-Steagall Act, and makes no effort to engage with the literature that refutes or supports its various explicit justifications. Our purpose is to explore a possible logic animating the integration of Glass-Steagall with the other New Deal banking reforms contained in the Banking Act of 1933, in light of the "finance-as-servant" perspective developed throughout this book. The preceeding analysis considers the potentially conflicting imperatives faced by the architects of New Deal banking reform, and makes the case that the Banking Act of 1933, the Glass-Steagall Act in particular, attempted to manage the simultaneous necessity of both stabilizing and enhancing commercial bank profitability while creating conditions that mitigated upward pressure on the cost of securing investment capital. In this sense, we argue that New Deal banking reforms are consistent with the subsequent creation of Keynesian welfare state capitalism. The intent here is not to serve as a partisan for the virtues of Glass-Steagall (nor to defend the justifications for Glass-Steagall that were publicly offered in the early 1930s), but to make a case that inter-capitalist bargaining power issues play a role in understanding the regulatory framework devised at the dawn of the New Deal.

Perhaps the longevity of the Glass-Steagall framework, and the New Deal banking reforms in general, are a testament to the relative dexterity with which these reforms navigated this perilous terrain of potentially inimical imperatives. Following World War II and its aftermath, the US economy enjoyed a prolonged period of economic growth and stability that is often referred to as the golden age of Keynesian welfare state capitalism. During that golden age, New Deal banking reforms presided over a period of relative tranquility in the financial sector, noteworthy in that bank profitability was relatively high and stable, bank failures became uncommon, and credit was forthcoming from the commercial banking system at relatively low real interest rates. Thus despite the constraints imposed by New Deal banking reforms, financial capital acquiesced to that regulatory framework:

> Although the reform legislation of the 1930s had divided up the financing terrain in what some thought was an arbitrary manner, the major financial intermediaries largely acceded to the legislation; it appeared

to offer both an umbrella of protection against the well-remembered wrath of the public after the profligate 1920s and an effective barrier to unwelcome competition. With each group's designated business territory in the financing landscape growing comfortably, there was little incentive to encroach on the territory of the other financial intermediaries and thereby disturb the unspoken *"pax financus"* that appeared to be serving everybody reasonably well (Hayes 1987, 3).

However, strains in the New Deal financial regulatory framework surfaced as American Keynesian welfare state capitalism began its decline. Chapter 6 presents the case that the contradictory imperatives that animated this framework ultimately unleashed forces that undermined it. The Glass-Steagall Act, in combination with other provisions of the Banking Acts, necessarily contained provisions which conferred differential advantages and disadvantages to financial capitalist firms in different regulatory classifications. Thus this financial regulatory structure contained within it the possibility that internecine struggles among financial capitalist firms might be ignited if conditions shifted in such a way that they gained incentives to undermine this pastiche of advantages and disadvantages.

In this sense, the complex impacts on competition among financial intermediaries were both the great strength and great weakness of the New Deal financial regulatory structure. To their credit, New Dealers did a commendable job of navigating the perils of potentially divergent agendas in a context in which the overall project of economic recovery demanded that none of them could be overlooked. But in keeping with our emphasis on contradiction, the strengths of the regulatory framework were also its weaknesses. The multiple effects of the Glass-Steagall framework on competition among financial intermediaries set the stage for competitive struggles that would eventually undermine it, along with other New Deal banking reforms. As time passed and competitive incentives changed with the evolving context of Keynesian welfare state capitalism, financial capitalist firms found ample reason and opportunity to attack the regulatory framework.

Chapter Six

From *Pax Financus* to *Bellum Financus:* The Contradictions of New Deal Banking Reform and the Transformation of US Finance

After a long "golden age" of relative economic growth and stability, Keynesian welfare state capitalism faced intensifying crises. While the viability of welfare state capitalism was being challenged, the American financial landscape was being transformed. This chapter reconsiders this financial transformation during the dénouement of welfare state capitalism via the contradictory imperatives implied in the "finance as servant" proposition. Preceding chapters argued that the New Deal financial regulatory framework confronted contradictory imperatives in order to both promote commercial bank profitability and create conditions conducive to the availability of investment capital on attractive terms. This chapter will make the case that, despite their adroit handling of these contractions, New Deal banking reforms also set in motion pressures in the form of competitive struggles among financial capitalist firms (and others). As these pressures intensified, *pax financus* devolved into *bellum financus,* and Glass-Steagall's financial compartmentalization became increasingly unsustainable and was ultimately repealed in 1999.

Chapter 5 argued that New Deal banking reforms responded to the "finance-as-servant" dilemma via financial compartmentalization. But while this compartmentalization contributed to the *pax financus* that prevailed in the golden age of Keynesian welfare state capitalism, it also sowed the seeds of its own destruction. Regulatory compartmentalization necessarily bestows an uneven assortment of advantages and disadvantages on the various categories of financial capitalist firms. If financial capitalist firms in one compartment discern competitive advantages enjoyed by firms of a different regulatory category, the incentive exists for the relatively under-privileged firms to have these privileges extended to themselves or to under-mine those regulatory advantages enjoyed by others. By the same token, any regulatory requirement that burdens a given category of financial capitalist firms *vis-à-vis* other firms produces incentives for the disadvantaged firms to attempt to evade or eliminate these restrictions. This uneven assortment of both regulatory strictures and perquisites creates the possibility of inter-necine struggle among financial capitalist firms as they attempt to manip-ulate these competitive advantages or disadvantages created by financial compartmentalization.

Commercial banks were, in many ways, a privileged beneficiary of financial compartmentalization. Barriers to entry into commercial bank-ing and interest rate controls reduced the costs associated with attracting deposits. Deposit insurance and lender of last resort support insulated com-mercial banks from crisis and conferred unparalleled security on savings held as bank deposits. Thanks to these advantages, as well as their access to the payments system that enabled commercial banks to execute transac-tions, bank deposits were attractive to the public. Reliable access to plen-tiful and inexpensive funds in the first phase of financial intermediation provided propitious conditions for bank profitability. Indeed, the persis-tence of these rather halcyon conditions in banking created a growing per-ception that commercial banking was excessively coddled[1]:

> Most banks were [stodgy]. They didn't make risky loans, and the "spread" between their cost of funds and the interest rates they could charge their borrowers was relatively stable at three to four percentage points, leaving a satisfactory profit margin for the bank after the deduc-tion of "G&A" (general and administrative) expenses and loan losses. That was, after all, the purpose of restricting entry by making charters hard to get, and limiting the interest rates bank could pay their deposi-tors: the government wanted the bank to be stable and profitable. . . . on balance banking was a steady, routine business from the Roosevelt rescue in the depression to . . . 1968 (Mayer 1997, 16).

Although non-bank financial capitalist firms (referred to here as "non-banks") largely acquiesced to New Deal banking reforms during the tumul-tuous conditions of the Great Depression and the Second World War, the regulatory advantages that enhanced the profitability of commercial banks created incentives for non-banks to find ways to compete with commercial banks. As the crisis of Keynesian welfare state capitalism was becoming evi-dent in the 1970s, a confluence of many factors led non-banks to act on these incentives. Inflationary pressures and changing institutional arrangements (such as the decline and fall of the Bretton Woods system) reshaped competition among foreign and domestic financial capitalist firms.[2] The increasing intellectual rejection of Keynesianism legitimated attacks on regulatory constraints in finance and elsewhere. The evolution of computing and communications technology facilitated the development of sophisticated financial instruments designed to subvert regulatory restrictions.

These and other developments created opportunities for non-banks to compete with commercial banks in ways that ultimately produced severe and unsustainable strain on the New Deal financial regulatory framework.[3] Non-banks found ways of challenging commercial bank hegemony in both phases of financial intermediation. In return, commercial banks adapted their practices for both accessing funds, making loans, and earning other forms of income. As these competitive struggles unfolded, both banks and non-banks began to blur the line between commercial banking and other forms of financial capitalist activity. Even non-financial firms (such as automobile companies and General Electric) began to engage in financial activities that had previously been the purview of financial capitalist firms. By 1999, the Glass Steagall Act finally succumbed to mounting pressures, and the blending of commercial and investment banking (together with other financial capitalist activities) was again permitted.

THE COMPETITIVE STRATEGIES OF NON-BANKS

As inflation accelerated in the 1970s, New Deal interest rate controls were transformed from their intended role as an implicit subsidy to a competitive encumbrance for banks. Both Regulation Q nominal interest rates caps on savings accounts and the prohibition of interest on checking accounts became an increasingly onerous penalty for bank depositors. Since non-banks were not subject to interest rate controls, this created an opportunity for them to siphon savings away from the commercial banking system. Although non-banks incurred additional costs as they out-bid banks for access to savings, non-banks were not obligated to hold required reserves or pay deposit insurance premiums, thus a greater proportion of every dollar they attracted could be used to earn some form of income. In addition, non-banks were not bound by the legal prohibition on interstate banking or by the restrictions imposed on banks on the amount of lending that could be provided to an individual borrower or category of borrowers.

However non-banks faced other obstacles in their attempt to compete with banks over access to savings in the first phase of financial intermediation. To some extent, depositors were compensated for forgone interest income by the deposit insurance and checking privileges offered by bank deposits. In order to provide a close substitute to deposits, non-banks sought ways of providing a measure of security comparable to deposit insurance and ways to replicate the capacity to execute transactions comparable to checking accounts.[4] Thus non-banks developed financial innovations and sought regulatory changes that would enable them to mimic these features of deposits and thereby mount a competitive assault on commercial banks.

A few examples illustrate the ways in which non-banks mimicked the security and checking privileges of bank deposits. In 1971, money market mutual funds (MMMF) were introduced as a mutual fund specializing in buying money market assets such as US Treasuries.[5] Money market assets paid interest rates in excess of the Regulation Q maximum, but their large denominations were impractical for small savers.[6] By operating as a mutual fund MMMFs overcame this obstacle. While they are not eligible for deposit insurance, the low default risk of assets such as US Treasuries is comparable to the security of an insured deposit. MMMFs also competed with traditional checking accounts in that they allowed shareholders to write checks (with some restrictions) against their MMMF shares. As nominal interest rates climbed above the Regulation Q cap in the late 1970s, MMMFs grew dramatically.[7] Moreover, MMMFs created opportunities for further financial innovations. For example, in 1977, Merrill Lynch developed cash management accounts (CMA). Previously investment income earned by investment bank customers was typically deposited into a commercial bank. Cash management accounts allowed investment banks to automatically invest these funds into a MMMF on behalf of their customers. These cash management accounts later evolved to offer check-writing privileges, credit cards, and loans.

Pension funds were another type of non-bank financial capitalist firm that encroached upon banks' capacity to attract deposits. Pension funds had previously been a problematic vehicle in which to store savings, but concerns about their safety were overcome with the passage of the Employee Retirement Income Security Act (ERISA) in 1974.[8] ERISA established the Pension Benefit Guaranty Corporation (PBGC), which provided limited insurance for employer-provided defined-benefit pension plans and elevated standards for their funding and diversification. Both the increased perceived safety of pension funds and ERISA requirements forcing employers to make substantial ongoing contributions to their defined-benefit pension plans encouraged a great inflow of resources into them. Prior to 1974, the total reserves held by pension funds amounted to slightly more than 50 percent of the deposits of commercial banks.[9] In the ten years following the passage of ERISA, the total reserves of pension funds grew by 145 percent and by 1984, savings held in pension funds exceeded those held in deposits. By the mid 1990s, about two dollars were held in pension funds for every dollar held in checking or savings accounts.

A defined-benefit pension plan exposes the employer to the possibility that the plan's assets may not generate sufficient funds to cover pension liabilities. Defined-contribution plans shift this risk onto pension recipients, but they are not eligible for PBGC coverage. In 1982, the federal government was prevailed upon to provide these plans with tax deferred status (see Kimpel 1997, 256). Preferential tax treatment made the lack of government-sponsored insurance for defined-contribution plans more attractive.[10] This created a tremendous opportunity for mutual funds, since defined-contribution plans provided increased capacity to direct the composition of the assets in these plans, and mutual funds enable savers to diversify even relatively modest holdings.

The success of non-banks in both paying higher rates of return than deposits and offering savings vehicles that approximated the security and accessibility of deposits (or compensated savers in some other manner) attacked the ability of commercial banks to attract funds via checking and savings accounts. Despite the efforts of banks to stave off this competitive threat (see below), the ultimate success of non-banks in luring savings out of deposits is illustrated in Figure 13. Figure 13 displays Federal Reserve's *Flow of Funds* data concerning the percentage of the total financial assets of households, non-profit organizations, and non-farm non-financial corporate business[11] that are held in various forms. Readers should note that, because of the categories used in *Flow of Funds,* the depiction of "deposits" displayed in this figure is an overstatement, thus the decline in savings and checking deposits is more precipitous than is suggested by this figure.[12] Despite the exaggeration of the size of deposits in the Figure 13, it provides an indication of the waning importance of commercial banks deposits especially after the mid-1980s.

The New Deal financial regulatory framework was predicated on the assumption that commercial banks intermediated the bulk of domestic savings, although they could only channel these savings to firms requiring investment capital in the form of bank loans. But the success of non-banks in transforming the first phase of financial intermediation created opportunities to transform the second phase as well. As non-banks increasingly succeeded in draining savings out of the banking system, they were poised to become a more prominent supplier of investment capital

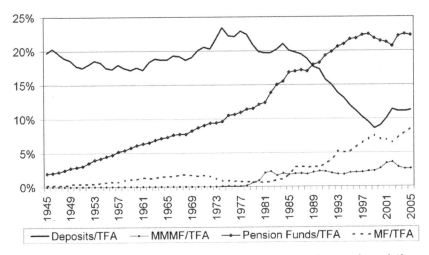

Figure 13. "Deposits," MMMFs, Pension Fund Reserves and Mutual Fund Shares as a Percentage of the Total Financial Assets of Households, Non-Profit Organizations and Non-Financial Corporate Business.

Source: *Flow of Funds*, Tables B.100 and B.102

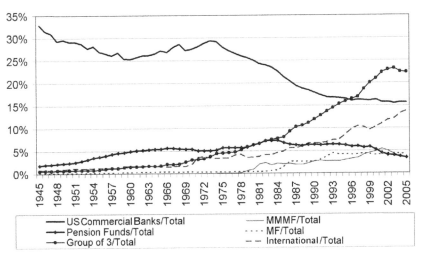

Figure 14. The Total Credit Market Assets of Commercial Banks, Pension Funds, MMMFs, Mutual Funds, Group of Three (GSE, Agency- and GSE-backed Mortgage Pools, ABS Issuers) and International Investors to Total Credit Market Assets, 1945–2005.

Source: *Flow of Funds*.

in its various forms. In the later part of the 1990s, pension funds held over half of their total financial assets as corporate equities, while for mutual funds this ratio was close to three quarters.[13] Figure 14 displays the percentage of total credit market assets[14] held by various types of financial capitalist firms. Until 1980, commercial banks held in excess of 25 percent of all credit market assets,[15] while by the time of the elimination of Glass-Steagall in 1999, commercial banks provided only 16 percent of it. At the same time, a variety of financial capitalist firms including both firms we have previously analyzed (mutual funds, money market mutual funds and pension funds) as well as other domestic (government-sponsored enterprises—such as Fannie Mae—agency and government-sponsored enterprise-backed mortgages pools and asset-backed securities issuers) and international entities made use of the proliferation of financial innovations to assume an important presence in US credit markets.

The growing pool of savings that was intermediated outside of the commercial banking system enlarged the ways in which productive capitalist firms could access funds. Firms in need of funds might be unable or unwilling to access them by issuing securities; if so, they are likely to be dependent on bank loans. One alternative to securities issuance is commercial paper, an uncollateralized short-term debt. Provided that commercial paper has a short maturity, it is not legally considered to be a security and thus avoids the requirements of the Securities and Exchange Commission. But the absence of some of the safeguards required in securities markets, and the fact that commercial paper is not secured by any specific asset, have meant that the commercial paper market has periodically erupted into crisis as a default by a commercial paper issuer ignites a panic analogous to a bank run. As purchasers of commercial paper disappear, issuers are obliged to collectively find other sources of funds. Following a convulsion in 1970,[16] the instability in the commercial paper was greatly attenuated, ironically with the assistance of commercial banks. Banks were enticed to earn fee income by providing lines of credit[17] to enable issuers of commercial paper to honor their debts during adverse circumstances. This contrived substitute for lender of last resort support enhanced stability in the commercial paper market, and enabled it to grow enormously as mutual funds, pension funds, and many others came forth as eager purchasers of commercial paper, and firms in need of funds turned to commercial paper as an alternative to bank loans (see Figure 15). In 1970, commercial paper outstanding constituted only about 10 percent of the commercial bank loans outstanding, but by the late 1990s commercial paper outstanding constituted 40 percent of the commercial bank loans outstanding.

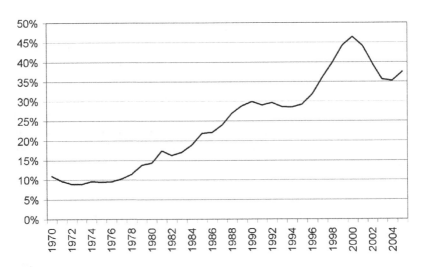

Figure 15. Commercial Paper Outstanding as a Percentage of Total Commercial Bank Loans Outstanding, 1970–2005.

Source: *Flow of Funds.*

COMMERCIAL BANK RESPONSES TO COMPETITION BY NON-BANKS

Banks pursued many strategies to counter non-banks' success in both diverting savings out of deposits[18] and encroaching on banks as a provider of funds. In terms of the first phase of financial intermediation, banks sought to enhance the attractiveness of deposits and attract funds via avenues other than deposits. In terms of the second phase of financial intermediation, banks both adapted their lending practices and sought new ways of earning income outside of the traditional practice of accepting deposits and making loans. However, these responses to the competition from non-banks had consequences for the stability of the commercial banking system. In part, banks responded by incurring increased risk, a competitive strategy encouraged by the moral hazard that animates the relationship between commercial banks and the state. Both because of the importance of deposit insurance as a remaining advantage that rested with the commercial banking system, and because of their explicit access to lender of last resort support (particularly among banks perceived to be "too big to fail"), commercial banks could entertain competitive strategies that might otherwise have been judged to be excessively risky. Thus banks' response to the competitive encroachment of non-banks had consequences for the overall stability of the commercial banking system.

To buttress their access to savings, commercial banks were obliged to subvert the interest rate controls that were originally enacted to support their profitability. For example, "sweep" accounts were developed to move funds from a checking account to an overnight repurchase agreement[19] to enable depositors to earn income on their checking accounts.[20] Commercial banks also sought ways around the Regulation Q cap on the interest rates payable on savings accounts. An illustration of this is the certificate of deposit (CD), which provides interest payments and the return of the principal at maturity in a manner analogous to a bond. However, retail CDs are classified as small time deposits,[21] and are thus covered by deposit insurance. In the early 1970s, commercial banks successfully lobbied for CDs to be freed from Regulation Q limits altogether. Thanks to these developments, the CD market grew ten-fold between 1965 and 1975 (Meerschwam 1987, 79).

However, the successful circumvention of interest rate controls presented banks with an additional dilemma in that it implied that they were incurring greater expense to attract deposits, as Figure 16 illustrates. To compensate for this increased expense, banks sought to increase the earning potential of deposits. Since required reserves represent a forgone opportunity to make new loans (and they do not earn interest at the Federal Reserve), banks continued their efforts to reduce their reserve holdings. To the extent that a checking account could be reclassified as a savings account, the bank would both economize on reserves (since savings accounts carry lower reserve requirements) and evade the prohibition on paying interest on checking accounts. This strategy was exemplified by the introduction of Negotiable Order of Withdrawal (NOW) accounts, which offer check-like privileges on accounts that are not categorized as transactions accounts. Banks lobbied to have reserve requirements diminished, and in 1980 the Depository Institutions Deregulation and Monetary Control Act (DIDMCA) both lowered reserve requirements[22] and phased out Regulation Q over a period of 6 years.[23] As a consequence of both financial innovations and regulatory change, the reserve holdings of the commercial banking system were dramatically reduced as a proportion of the total financial assets held by commercial banks (see Figure 17). But as required reserves were reduced, this mechanism intended to stabilize the banking system became increasingly ineffectual.

In their strategies to stem their diminished deposit holdings, banks also sought to compete for funds by taking greater advantage of their access to the government safety net. For example, "brokered deposits" were developed

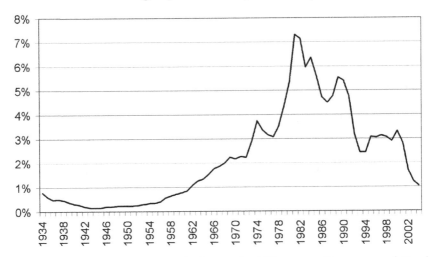

Figure 16. Interest on Deposits in Domestic Offices as a Percentage of Total Domestic Deposits of FDIC Member Banks, 1934–2002.

Source: *Historical Statistics on Banking.*

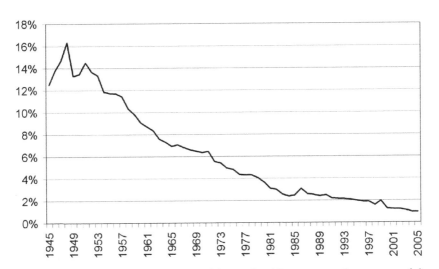

Figure 17. Vault Cash and Reserves Held at Federal Reserve as a Percentage of the Total Financial Assets of US-Chartered Commercial Banks, 1945–2005.

Source: *Flow of Funds.*

to circumvent deposit insurance caps. Amounts in excess of the deposit insurance cap could be divided among many commercial banks so that each bank held only the maximum amount covered by the FDIC. In this way, the depositor was fully protected by deposit insurance despite the explicit cap on it. However, the temptation existed for troubled banks to pay a premium to gain access to brokered deposits in an attempt to earn their way out of imminent insolvency. If the imperiled bank was unsuccessful, the FDIC would be left to clean up the mess. By the early 1980s, this practice was becoming a concern for systemic stability, given that in some cases brokered deposits were in excess of 50 percent of the total liabilities of the failed bank.[24]

Alongside strategies to buttress their access to funds via traditional deposits, banks also sought to attract savings in other forms. In banking parlance, accessing savings in the first phase of financial intermediation in forms other than traditional deposits is called "purchasing" funds. Purchased funds were not subject to interest rate controls or reserve requirements, nor were they eligible for deposit insurance. One of the landmarks in the use of purchased funds by commercial banks was Citibank's development of the large negotiable CDs in 1961. These "wholesale" CDs are usually denominated in amounts of $1 million or more, and are often purchased by institutional investors seeking a small premium over Treasury bills. Other forms of purchased funds include repurchase agreements,[25] commercial paper issued by a commercial bank via its holding company,[26] and borrowing in the Euromarket.

Banks' attempts to intermediate savings via purchased funds also had potentially destabilizing consequences. In the past, the time that elapsed between the initial suspicions of a bank's possible failure and the onslaught of depositor withdrawals provided banks and regulators with valuable reaction time. As they can be instantly removed through electronic channels by large, well-informed institutions that react quickly to information (as well as rumors[27]) about problems in a bank, purchased funds are viewed as the "hot money" of bank funding (Sinkey 2002, 105).[28] A bank that is reliant on purchased funds can find itself virtually shut out of purchased funds markets if it is thought to be in imminent difficulty. The failure of Continental Illinois[29] epitomizes this concern about the role of purchased funds and bank instability, but Continental was by no means unusual among large US commercial banks in its heavy use of purchased funds.[30]

Banks' increasing reliance on purchased funds created pressure for government intervention to avert or resolve banking crises with large purchased funds components, since a disruption in the markets in which banks purchase funds could provoke systemic instability. But the government safety net was not designed for a banking system dependent on purchased funds. Purchased funds are typically not explicitly covered by deposit insurance. Moreover, deposit insurance was designed to deter legions of small depositors from withdrawing their funds, hence an upper cap was appropriate. This cap is not sufficient to avert an electronic funds run.

Creditors in purchased funds markets must be assured that their funds are protected in their entirety. Thus in the case of Continental Illinois, the FDIC was forced to guarantee that all its depositors and other general creditors would be "fully protected," regardless of the cap on deposit insurance and despite the fact that a number of the liabilities in question were not insurable deposits (FDIC 1997, 244).[31] This not only increases the expense of resolving bank failures, it represents an expansion of the government safety net beyond banking *per se*. Non-banks (as well as other types of firms) purchase funds, thus to the extent that the government safety net is stretched to address crises emanating from activities linked to the purchase of funds, this represents a movement towards the provision of emergency assistance to financial capitalist activities in general—so long as a given crisis provokes concerns that the commercial banking system is in danger of destabilization.

In terms of the second phase of financial intermediation, banks were under pressure as large corporate borrowers with good credit ratings increasingly accessed funds elsewhere. This compelled banks to lend to riskier borrowers. Commercial bank lending to less-developed countries (LDCs)[32] expanded to the extent that the nine largest US commercial banks had advanced loans to LDCs that constituted 288 percent of their bank capital by the end of 1982 (Sachs and Huizinga 1987, 558).[33] This strategy turned sour as the high interest rates in the early 1980s made it impossible for Mexico (and other debtor countries) to meet its debt service commitments in 1982.[34] Over the next five years, commercial banks were able to manage this crisis, thanks in part to regulatory permissiveness that allowed the banks to count as current income the interest payments made as a result of "involuntary" loans made to the debtor in order to cover interest obligations and thereby prevent outright default (see Sachs and Huizinga 1987, 557). By some accounts, this regulatory forbearance was necessary lest seven or eight of the ten largest US banks fall into official insolvency (FDIC 1997, 207).[35] Meanwhile, in the 1980s commercial banks extended their lending to activities connected with commercial real estate, mergers and acquisitions, and the oil and gas sectors, all of which are typically regarded as risky lending areas.[36] Problems ensued with real estate loans, as they had been advanced on the strength of the underlying collateral rather than on the borrower's ability to generate earnings from the asset.[37] A collapse in commercial real estate, particularly in New England, had disastrous implications for commercial banks, and played a prominent role in the surge of bank failures in the late 1980s and early 1990s (see Figure 8).

Commercial banks also tried to generate income from activities other than extending loans. Non-interest income might be earned on activities connected with the operation of a deposit account (such as fees levied for using automatic banking machines). But fees were also increasingly generated as a by-product of new financial innovations designed to enhance commercial bank profitability under these onerous competitive circumstances. For example, to enable a given deposit base to support more lending, commercial banks began to securitize aspects of their loan portfolio. Securitization involves gathering together loans (usually of a given type, such as mortgages or credit card receivables), packaging them as securities, and selling the claims to the interest and/or principal payments to third parties. Securitized loans are removed from the bank's balance sheet, thus enabling the bank to fund new loans. If the bank retains the responsibility of servicing the loans, it earns a fee for such things as managing the collection of the payments on the loans that back the security. Various forms of non-interest income became increasingly important for commercial banks throughout the 1980s and 1990s (see Figure 18). While in 1960 commercial banks earned about 17 cents in non-interest income for every dollar of interest income earned, by the late 1990s this figure had risen to over 30 cents per dollar.

In many instances, this increasing reliance on fee income had troubling consequences for the stability of the banking system. For example,

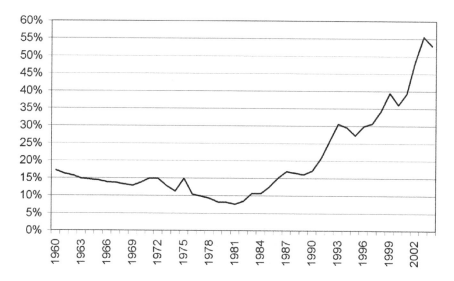

Figure 18. Non-Interest Income as a Percentage of Interest Income for FDIC-Insured Commercial Banks, 1960–2004.

Source: *Historical Statistics on Banking.*

the provision of lines of credit generates fee income.[38] Yet lines of credit can be destabilizing in that they are often activated when a would-be borrower faces difficulty, thereby forcing a bank to advance a loan when the likelihood of default on the loan is high. Firms in distress often activate lines of credit prior to their failure, as was the case when Enron obliged several large banks to honor their lines of credit prior to its collapse. If several firms tap their lines of credit simultaneously and subsequently fail (if, for example, firms in a certain industry or geographical region are simultaneously imperiled) this could be destabilizing to the commercial banking system. By acting as a lender of last resort to any entity that has a line of credit, banks themselves may require lender of last resort support. Thus the Federal Reserve is exposed to the possibility that it may be prevailed upon to be the *de facto* lender of last resort to non-bank firms via this mechanism.

Over time, banks earned income in activities that were increasingly distant from the traditional business of taking deposits and making loans. For example, commercial banks grew to have a prominent role as dealers of derivatives. Derivatives are a contract between two parties that confers either the necessity (in futures, forward, or swap contracts) or the possibility (in an option contract) of engaging in a buying/selling transaction in the future. The value of the contract is derived from the future values of some underlying variable, such as interest rates, exchange rates, equity or commodity prices, or the occurrence of a host of other economic or noneconomic events. For example, a bank may enter into an interest rate swap which pays a counterparty a fixed rate of interest, while that counterparty will pay the bank the prevailing rate on Treasury bills.[39] The dealer will build into this transaction some margin that constitutes its fee, but the dealer is also exposed to the possibility that the payout may be more than the value received from the counterparty, or that the counterparty may default entirely. Eager to partake of its lucrative aspects, US banks increased their derivatives activities at a compound annual rate of about 20 percent between 1990 and 1999, until by 1999 US commercial banks held derivatives contracts with a notional value of $33 trillion (Greenspan 1999).

The destabilizing potential of derivatives is perhaps most famously captured by Warren Buffet's description of them as "financial weapons of mass destruction," carrying dangers that, while now latent, are potentially lethal (Buffet 2002, 16). Derivatives dealers are exposed to credit risks, even for scrupulously "matched"[40] "over-the counter"[41] derivatives contracts. If one of the dealers' counterparties defaults, the derivatives dealer continues to be exposed to the necessity of fulfilling the terms of the contract for the other "matched" counterparty. The counterparty whose derivatives contract benefits the dealer may default, while the derivative contract that is costly to the dealer remains in force. This problem is intensified by inter-linkages and the high degree of leveraging[42] that characterize derivatives markets. In addition, derivative dealers may intentionally take a speculative position by refraining from balancing one derivatives contract with another matching derivative. These dangers help to explain why derivatives dealers are often housed within large banks.[43] As the failure of Long Term Capital Management suggests, banks regarded as "too big to fail" are better positioned to prevail upon the government to intervene if a crisis in derivatives markets threatens to become a systemic banking crisis.

Via a combination of these and other strategies, commercial banks attempted to fight back against the competitive onslaught of non-banks. Despite some success, the return on assets (ROA) of FDIC-member commercial banks decreased over time. While the ROA hovered between 0.75 percent and 0.88 percent from 1960 to 1973, by the early 1980s, it was a little over 0.6 percent. Bank profitability plummeted in 1987 (the year in which banks acknowledged their problems with third world debt—see below and above), but if banks had revealed these problems earlier the downward trend in ROA during the 1980s would have been more striking than is depicted in Figure 12. In 1986, nine US banks enjoyed a long-term triple A rating from Moody's, but by 1993, J.P. Morgan and Co. was the only bank left in this category (Mayer 1997, 220). Moreover, the increased risks taken by commercial banks to defend their profitability contributed to an accelerated incidence of bank failures. Before 1975, fewer than 10 FDIC-member banks failed per year. Bank failures exceeded 120 per year between 1985 and 1992, and in some years reached 200 or more (see Figure 8).

Legislators, regulators, and banks themselves have attempted to manage these new sources of instability. After much legal wrangling, the FIDC managed to put limits on brokered deposits.[44] Risk-based fees for deposit insurance were introduced in the 1991 Comprehensive Deposit Insurance Reform and Taxpayer Protection Act. As required reserves diminished, regulators moved toward capital-adequacy regulations on commercial banks. New financial instruments (such as credit derivatives) have been designed to offer protection in many activities. While these newer measures have contributed to commercial bank stability, they in turn set in motion other sources of instability. For example, the imposition of capital requirements has possible pro-cyclical implications. A reputable bank will be easily able to acquire new capital during prosperous times, which allows banks to expand lending (particularly in stock market booms when securing equity capital is relatively easy). However, a bank facing a crisis will have great difficulty acquiring new capital to stabilize its operations. Risk-based deposit insurance premiums[45] and credit derivatives[46] have also had unintended effects that may exacerbate instability in the commercial banking system and beyond.

THE EROSION OF COMPARTMENTALIZATION AND THE REPEAL OF THE GLASS STEAGALL ACT

The various changes in the financial sector that accelerated during the dénouement of the Keynesian welfare state created a wealth of opportunities to undermine the financial compartmentalization devised by the New Deal regulatory framework. Banks, non-banks, and even productive capitalist firms and others sought opportunities to transgress these boundaries. Each new transgression of the regulatory compartments reconfigured the competitive landscape and offered new possibilities to shift the relative bargaining power between productive and financial capitalist firms.

The flourishing commercial paper market facilitated the ability of finance companies to create what D'Arista and Schlesinger (1997) called a "parallel banking system." Finance companies had long existed as a type of financial capitalist firm that acquires funds and makes loans, often to consumers. Once the commercial paper market flourished in the 1970s, finance companies could sell commercial paper, thus freeing themselves from commercial bank loans as a means of accessing funds for subsequent re-lending. In this way, savings that were initially accessed by MMMFs or pension funds could be provided to finance companies that could then make any manner of loans (see Figure 19). Since finance companies were not highly regulated, they did not have to comply with the various soundness regulations and prohibitions on interstate banking that applied to commercial banks. A variety of productive capitalist firms, such as General Electric and automobile companies, developed prominent finance company subsidiaries.[47] While originally these "captive" finance companies focused on funding consumers' purchases from the parent firm, some finance companies (such as those associated with General Electric) became involved with providing investment capital to a wide variety of firms that might or might not be otherwise connected to the parent company. They also engaged in other types of financial capitalist activities, such as the provision of insurance. The evolution of finance companies not only transgressed financial compartmentalization, it also blurred the separation of finance and commerce and created a variety of possibilities (such as situations in which a productive capitalist firms makes loans to suppliers of inputs in return for pricing or other concessions) that violate the supposition that there is an arm's length relationship between the suppliers and users of investment capital.

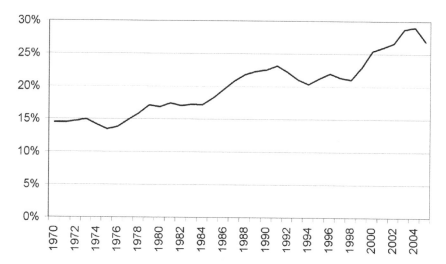

Figure 19. Total Financial Assets of Finance Companies as a Percentage of Total Financial Assets of US-Chartered Commercial Banks, 1970–1999.

Source: *Flow of Funds.*

However, the capacity to mix a full range of productive and financial capitalist activities was constrained to the extent that Glass-Steagall continued to prevent firms engaged in various financial capitalist activities from operating commercial banks.

Meanwhile, commercial banks also sought to diversify their activities into other financial capitalist or productive capitalist activities. This obliged banks to find some way to evade the prohibition on this diversification imposed by the Bank Holding Company Act (BHCA) of 1956. The BHCA defined a bank holding company as a firm that controlled two or more banks, yet in the 1960s commercial banks argued that a commercial bank residing in a holding company that controlled only one bank was exempt from BHCA restrictions. The resulting "one-bank holding companies" flourished until Congress acted to address this loophole that was creating opportunities for commercial bank involvement in diversified capitalist firms. In 1970 the Holding Company Act Amendments were passed, which allowed bank holding companies to exist, but their non-banking activities were to be "closely related to banking."

While this legislation limited commercial bank's ability to diversify, it had unintended consequences that assisted the formation of diversified capitalist firms in other respects. The 1970 legislation defined a commercial bank as a firm that 1) accepts demand deposits and 2) makes commercial loans. When lawyers successfully argued that a firm that does only one of these two activities is not legally a bank, the "non-bank bank" was born. In 1980, Gulf and Western's finance company subsidiary acquired Fidelity National Bank. The Comptroller of the Currency was persuaded that the resulting firm need not be classified as a bank in the meaning of the BHCA so long as it was divested of its commercial loan portfolio. The parent firm could use the fact that the non-bank bank had access to the payments system to execute transactions related to credit cards, consumer lending, and other activities, thereby removing the necessity of paying fees to commercial banks for clearing transactions (see Vietor 1987, 49–50). In addition, the non-bank banks could be housed within a corporate structure in which other subsidiaries were engaged in securities underwriting and insurance brokerage.

A battle ensued as the Federal Reserve moved to broaden the definition of a bank. In 1986, the United States Supreme Court struck down the changes in the definition of commercial banks that the Federal Reserve had imposed to address the growth of non-bank banks, and within weeks almost a hundred applications to form non-bank banks were filed. Insurance companies, mutual funds, brokerage firms, and even retailers like Sears began to run non-bank banks in competition with commercial banks.[48] In response to this rapid transformation of financial capitalist activity, the Competitive Equality in Banking Act (CEBA) was passed in 1987. Although the CEBA is primarily remembered for its intervention in the unfolding Savings and Loan crisis, it also placed more stringent requirements on non-bank banks.[49] Under the circumstances of the rapidly dissolving compartmentalization of finance, the CEBA revealed the increasing difficulty of constructing any definition of a commercial bank that related banks to the specificities of their role as financial intermediaries. CEBA expanded the definition of a bank to include any institution that is a member of the FDIC, thus acknowledging that conceptualizations of financial capitalist activity based on norms associated with New Deal compartmentalization were now anachronistic.

Over time, New Deal compartmentalization was becoming increasingly unsustainable. Regulations were being evaded or removed entirely, both in areas directly pertaining to Glass-Steagall restrictions and in other areas (such as interstate banking) that further changed the dynamics of competition among financial capitalist firms. A pervasive celebration of "de-regulation" as well as effective lobby efforts, persuaded regulators to refrain from taking actions that might have defended financial compartmentalization. Only a few of the highlights in the process of dismantling financial compartmentalization can be mentioned here. In 1986, the Federal Reserve Board was prevailed upon to reinterpret Section 20 of the Glass-Steagall Act, which prohibited commercial banks from being "engaged principally" in securities business. The Federal Reserve allowed banks to earn up to 5 percent of gross revenues from investment banking activities. Thereafter ensued battles concerning the interpretation of the phrase "engaged principally," and over time the 5 percent limit was increased and the types of investment banking activities that were permissible were broadened. By 1996 bank holding companies were permitted to own investment bank affiliates with up to 25 percent of their business in securities underwriting. In 1997, Banker's Trust became the first US bank to purchase an investment bank, and in 1998 the Travelers-Citicorp merger was announced. Since this merger blended insurance, commercial banking, and investment banking, it was in violation of the Glass-Steagall Act. The merger would have required the divestiture of some lines of business in the new firms within 2 years. However, Congress succumbed to intense lobbying and the Glass-Steagall Act was repealed in 1999.

With the repeal of the Glass Steagall Act in 1999 via the Financial Services Modernization Act (Gramm-Leach-Bliley Act), a "financial holding company" (FHC) could now combine commercial banking, investment banking, insurance provision, and other financial capitalist activities within one holding company structure. This provoked a round of mergers and acquisitions amongst large financial capitalist firms which transformed the financial sector in a manner reminiscent of the pre-New Deal era, when in the context of a stock market bubble financial capitalist firms rushed to blend commercial and investment banking.

The Gramm-Leach-Bliley Act did maintain some obstacles to the financial holding companies' capacity to engage in non-financial activity. While financial holding companies are permitted to take a controlling interest in non-financial enterprises,[50] these investments are not to be held indefinitely.[51] Moreover, the financial holding company is not intended to "routinely manage or operate" any non-financial firm in which it invests (see Kroszner, 2000). In due course, these restrictions on creating diversified capitalist firms are being challenged by financial holding companies. At the same time, other firms such as Wal-Mart are making inroads into banking via Industrial Loan Companies, a corporate structure that escapes restrictions placed on financial holding companies while qualifying for FDIC coverage (in some cases).

FINANCE AS MASTER?

The culmination of these competitive struggles has been a transformation of finance. This new era of "financialization" is vastly different from the rather circumscribed activities and institutions envisioned by the New Deal financial regulatory framework. Pervading the examination of this new era in finance are metaphors which stress the hegemony of finance. In contrast to the "finance as servant" paradigm, finance is now "master": "What happened in the Roaring Nineties was that a set of longstanding checks and balances—a balance between Wall Street, Main Street . . . and labor, between Old Industry and New Technology, government and the market—was upset, in some essential ways, by the new ascendancy of Finance. Everyone deferred to its judgment" (Stiglitz 2003, xiv).

However, our analysis refrains from declaring contemporary finance as either master or servant. We have focused on the "finance as servant" proposition in terms of the question of the relative bargaining power of productive and financial capitalist firms as it relates to the access of investment capital. (We thus left aside many other important questions, such as the impacts of financialization on stability or inequality.) Given our emphasis on the master/servant analytic via this bargaining power approach, we concede that the various developments discussed above—and others—had multiple and diverse impacts on bargaining power between productive and financial capital. In some respects, new developments among financial capitalist firms provoked more vigorous competition in the second phase of financial intermediation. This diminished the bargaining power of financial capitalist firms vis-à-vis productive capitalist firms. However, the breaches of financial compartmentalization that facilitated the development of diversified financial capitalist firms supported the bargaining power of financial capitalists. In particular, the creation of diversified financial capitalist firms anchored by commercial banks marks an opportunity to reconfigure this bargaining power in the favor of financial capitalist firms. Meanwhile the increasingly international arena in which productive and financial capitalist encounter each other, as well as a myriad of other developments in financial instruments and regulatory practices, have many varied influences on the relative bargaining power of finance and production.

However, the analysis of the bargaining relationship between productive and financial capitalists throughout this book is undertaken on the assumption of an arm's length relationship between productive and financial capitalist. As productive capitalist firms have diversified into a variety of types of financial capitalist activities, FHCs seek to expand the kinds of activities they are permitted to undertake, and other mechanisms are developed by which non-financial capitalist firms might enter banking, the separation between commerce and finance becomes increasingly blurred. Just as the New Deal's somewhat arbitrary compartments among financial capitalist firms were subjected to attack when circumstances unfolded which produced compelling incentives to do so, the somewhat arbitrary lines between commerce and finance could be subject to attack should that portend lucrative opportunities. If the erosion of this line between commerce and finance gathers momentum, we may revisit Hilferding's "finance capital" in the form of large conglomerates blending all manner of capitalist activities. The New Dealers contended with this possiblity in terms of the specter of the "money-trust." But as New Dealer Adolph Berle cautions, it is a perennial possiblity:

> In every generation concern has arisen, sometimes to the boiling point. Fear has emerged that the United States might one day discover that a relatively small group of individuals, especially through banking institutions they headed, might become virtual masters of the economic destiny of the United States (in Markham, 2002 Frontmatter)

There is no necessity that production and finance will be united under the dominant influence of "finance capital." Any number of circumstances may arise that both impede or support this possibility, and there are no conclusive means of assessing which influences will prevail in the future. But this possiblity is always latent. As the experience of the New Deal banking regulation suggests, even a regulatory framework that appears stable and inviolate for a long period can succumb to the contradictory imperatives that animate it. Given that this book is motivated to support the pursuit of economic alternatives, a consideration of the possible implications of this latent possiblity may be useful if political opportunities to intervene should arise.

Chapter Seven

New Deal Banking Reforms and Future Alternative Economic Agendas

Our reconsideration of the New Deal financial regulatory framework and its role in American welfare state capitalism is not intended solely for those with a retrospective interest in the political economy of financial regulation. Since it shapes the ways in which our collective savings are deployed to promote various economic ends, financial intermediation is a perpetual concern for advocates of alternative economic agendas. Given the capacity of financial intermediaries to both help and hinder economic developments that differ from the status quo, the future pursuit of alternative economic agendas can benefit from insights gleaned from the New Deal's experience with domestic banking reform as a component of a project of economic reform.

This retrospective examination does not conclude with any ready-made blueprints for future financial reforms. We have not developed a case either for or against some re-implementation or adaptation of the Glass-Steagall Act or other New Deal regulatory measures. Conditions have certainly changed so dramatically that any attempt to emulate these measures in hopes of reinstating the *pax financus* that prevailed during the golden age of the Keynesian welfare state would be faced with enormous challenges. But even while analyzing the New Deal banking reforms in their own historical context, we have refrained from either endorsing or condemning these particular financial regulations. While our analysis has argued that they showed considerable ingenuity in navigating the contradictory imperatives they faced, we have also discussed how these same contradictions nevertheless contributed to the ultimate demise of the New Deal financing regulatory framework.

If no judgment is offered on the merits and demerits of financial compartmentalization for future financial regulatory endeavors, what guidance is offered in terms of a suggested course for future action? It is hoped that the preceeding analysis provokes critical reflection on alternative economic agendas themselves. To this end, we conclude by illustrating how some of the insights garnered from this re-examination of banking reform in the New Deal may raise important questions for future projects that challenge the economic status quo.

ATTENTION TO CONTRADICTION AND THE PURSUIT OF ECONOMIC ALTERNATIVES

One recurrent emphasis throughout this analysis is the omnipresence of contradiction. As the brief consideration of dialectics in Chapter 1 discussed, the emphasis on mutually constitutive interaction indicates that any policy intervention will provoke its negation. But if contradiction is ubiquitous, what then is the contribution of this study of New Deal financial architecture? It illustrates that New Deal financial regulatory framework was animated by contradictions, but from the initial endorsement of the logic of mutual constitutivity it follows that everything is necessarily contradictory. However salutary (or not) we may deem the intended goal of the policy intervention, however efficacious (or not) we may deem the policy in achieving its stated objectives during some given time span, all policy intervention will set in motion forces that undermine it. There may be a multitude of criteria that lead one to prefer this or that policy intervention or to judge a given policy intervention as more or less successful, but no policy framework can claim to have transcended contradiction. Just as New Deal banking regulation was animated by contradictions, so will any future project of financial reform seeking to promote economic alternatives.

If all intervention is contradictory, does this perspective counsel inaction? On the contrary, since this perspective insists that contradictory dynamics animate both action and inaction, refraining from action provides no refuge from the implications of contradiction. Even the most *laissez-faire* opposition to regulatory intervention will encounter pressures that compel further regulation.[1] Both advocates for and against regulatory activism confront a ceaseless cycle in which financial regulation provokes impulses for deregulation, which in turn stimulate demands for re-regulation.

If immunity from contradiction is impossible, how should advocates of alternative economic agendas proceed? While this analysis deprives the reader of any hope of formulating some optimal policy that can escape contradiction, perhaps some other hope may take its place. The embrace of contradiction has liberating implications, insofar as it frees critics of the status quo from repetitive and irresolvable obligations. Alternative economic agendas have routinely devised policy proposals that are roundly discredited as inferior and impractical relative to the policies that support the status quo. This is no great surprise, given that the evaluative criteria which condemn alternative economic agendas are often those criteria that look favorably upon the economic status quo. No trans-theoretical metric is available that can declare any given policy unambiguously superior to its alternatives.[2] Even within the confines of a given theoretical paradigm, our emphasis on contradiction implies that all policies both promote and detract from their stated objective. The policies that support the economic status quo are not more or less subject to contradictory dynamics than the policies that challenge the status quo.

This book is motivated by the hope that an emphasis on contradiction enlarges the political space in which alternatives may be discussed. We might immediately concede that "our" policies are contradictory. They pursue certain ends that we find desirable, and they are also prone to destabilizing forces, likely to provoke attacks, etc. The same claims can be made about "their" policies. Thus this embrace of contradiction has the potential to free advocates of alternative economic agendas of having to fight battles that cannot be won. We need not postpone action indefinitely in hopes that the continuous refinement of an alternative economic agenda's policy mix can ever surmount the charge that it is contradictory. This is not to obviate the necessity of critical analysis and debate about economic alternatives and the means to pursue them. On the contrary, this book is one such exercise of subjecting a given policy intervention to scrutiny to anticipate its contradictory dynamics in a particular constellation of circumstances. But this acceptance of contradiction within a perspective of mutual constitutivity does dispense with the vain efforts to justify intervention on the basis of some incontrovertible "proof" of its optimality, guarantees of its stability, or other such promises.

The rejection of policy optimality and the embrace of contradiction offer an intriguing possiblity. If there is no trans-theoretical justification establishing the optimality of any given policy intervention, and no policy intervention transcends contradiction, on what basis may we act? With no unassailable criteria available, we are open to persuasion. A case must be made for some given course of action, and that case is adjudicated by any number of criteria. We may argue on behalf of our preferred evaluative criteria, but we are not at liberty to impose them. And since no options are excluded *a priori* from consideration, political space is enlarged for debate. The immutability of given economic arrangements is thrown into question: we move from the paralyzing mantra that "there is no alternative" to the possibility that there is nothing but alternatives.

ALTERNATIVE ECONOMIC AGENDAS

The analysis presented in this book depicts New Deal economic reforms as a pro-investment agenda crafted in the context of a widespread growing repudiation of the economic status quo during the Great Depression. New Dealers responded via government action intended to preserve capitalism while moderating what was viewed as its most objectionable characteristics. These arrangements evolved into what Paul Krugman has described as the 'Keynesian compact': "In effect, capitalism and its economists made a deal with the public: it will be okay to have free markets from now on, because we know enough to prevent any more Great Depressions" (1999, 103). Those persuaded of the omnipresence of contradictions look askance at the mollifying assurances offered in such "deals." Under some circumstances, periods of relative stability are possible (particularly if political and other contextual circumstances support vigorous actions to forestall destabilizing tensions from surfacing). But contextual circumstances are ceaselessly changing, raising the perpetual possiblity that the shifting context may reconfigure incentives in a manner that unleashes developments that negate that relative stability.

Indeed, there is no necessity that the "Keynesian compact" is the preferred option for advocates of alternative economic agendas. It is hoped that the preceeding discussion of the implications of contradiction emboldens many far-reaching questions concerning the economic attributes we seek to encourage. Is investment our preferred goal? Do we endorse other economic objectives rather than or alongside investment? Even if investment is among our objectives, we may ask whether all types of investment are desirable. Might we wish to promote certain kinds of investment activities over others? Must the firms that invest be capitalist firms?

The debates concerning these issues will in turn reshape our *desiderata* vis-à-vis financial intermediation. How might financial intermediation be shaped to support the sorts of economic activity we prefer? In what ways does financial intermediation shape the relative bargaining power of various economic actors? What interventions might be possible that enhance the bargaining power of those economic actors engaging in the activities we prefer? Many of the contradictory dynamics discussed throughout this book emanated from the situation in which financial intermediation is carried on by financial capitalist firms. Given that all dimensions of alternative economic projects are open to scrutiny, we may question the implications of challenging financial intermediation as a capitalist activity.

We are invited to interrogate any and all economic attributes we may have previously viewed as necessary, "better," or otherwise beyond debate. But this invitation is not accompanied by any comforting assurances that this interrogation will generate options that transcend contradiction. On the contrary, the pursuit of such certainty is illusory. Whatever economic attributes we might seek to change, new contradictions will surface. If economic goals other than investment are endorsed, or if financial intermediaries or other firms were to be organized on some other basis than capitalist firms, or if any other prevailing economic arrangements are challenged, these new arrangements would also be animated by multiple and conflicting objectives that would present both opportunities and perils for alternative economic agendas. Our attentiveness to contradictory dynamics may support us in anticipating and analyzing these dynamics as they unfold, but it cannot abolish them.

The New Deal and its banking reforms were facilitated because, in that particular context, public debate entertained ambitious and unconventional. Many of these proposals would have been widely regarded as illegitimate or impractical just a few years before Roosevelt took office. Of course, the circumstances of the time encouraged such boldness, but circumstances may again cause broad-based reflection on the role of finance and the types of economic outcomes that contemporary finance generates.

One never knows what circumstances will create the opportunity to advance alternative economic agendas. Amongst the many potential reasons that finance may increasingly become the focus of critical scrutiny are the reemergence of diversified capitalist firms reminiscent of Hilferding's description in *Finance Capital*. Should the emergence of large firms blending all manner of capitalist activity promote economic outcomes that are widely unpopular, this might create opportunities to revisit financial regulation. And if antipathy towards finance brings public concern to, in Adolph Berle's words, the "boiling point" (in Markham, 2002 Frontmatter), it may provide opportunities for much more wide-ranging reconsideration of the economic status quo.

Notes

NOTES TO CHAPTER ONE

1. See for example Bello, Bullard and Malhotta (2000); Eatwell and Taylor (2000); Epstein (ed.) (2005); Blackburn (2006); and Stockhammer (2004).
2. In addition, advocates of various forms of alternative economic arrangements are attracted to the welfare state insofar as it engaged in such measures as income redistribution and the targeted support of various disadvantaged sections of the population.
3. Mundell claimed that international capital mobility, independent domestic monetary policy and stable exchange rates could not occur simultaneously (1962). Fleming published seperately on the trilemma.
4. See for example Alexander, Dhumale and Eatwell (2006); Eatwell and Taylor (2000); D'Arista (2000), Eatwell and Taylor (eds.) (2002); Eichengreen (1994 and 2006); Epstein (ed.) (2005); and Palley (2006).
5. A variety of heterodox economists consider various dimensions of domestic financial architecture in ways that overlap with certain aspects of our investigation of domestic financial regulation (see D'Arista (1993); Henwood (1998); Dymski and Pollin (eds.) (1994); and Minsky (1986)). There is an important literature on the contrasts between so-called "bank-based" financial systems versus "capital market-based" systems, but this literature has been shaped largely by its application to the question of the role of financial systems in developing countries (for an overview of this literature on "national financial complexes," see Grabel (1997)). Another body of literature that takes up the question of the domestic financial arrangements during the American welfare state is the one connected with the social structure of accumulation analyses (see for example Wolfson (1994); and Isenberg (2000)).
6. New Deal reforms are characterized here as pro-capitalist in that New Dealers explicitly understood the American economy as capitalist and they sought to save this economic system rather than dismantle it. Thus we forgo the lively debates pursued in various theoretical traditions concerning the precise definition of capitalism. Within these debates, various criteria are often taken as distinguishing features of capitalism: the presence or absence

of exploitative class processes; the pervasiveness of market allocation; the private ownership of the means of production are among the most often cited. Whatever impacts the New Deal had on these various attributes of the American economy, it did not dismantle them.

7. Other prominent New Deal financial reforms include the Securities Act of 1933, the Home Loan Owners' Act of 1933, the Securities Exchange Act of 1934, the Public Utility Holding Act of 1935, the Federal Credit Union Act of 1934, the Banking Act of 1935 (see discussion below), the Maloney Act of 1938, and the Investment Company Act of 1940, as well as several amendments to tax laws.

8. The Glass-Steagall Act is usually considered to be sections 16, 20, 21 and 32 of the Banking Act of 1933.

9. In May of 1932 Roosevelt echoed an analysis in the under consumptionist vein when he explained the depression as follows: "No, our basic trouble is not an insufficiency of capital. It was insufficient distribution of buying power coupled with an oversufficient speculation in production. While wages rose in many of our industries, they did not as a whole rise proportionately to the reward to capital, and at the same time the purchasing power of the great groups of our population was permitted to shrink" (Roosevelt 1966, 79).

10. Indeed Keynes declared in 1927 that his kinship with Institutionalist John. R. Commons was such that "there seems to me to be no other economist with whose general way of thinking I feel myself in such general accord" (in Atkinson and Oleson 1998, 1019).

11. For example, Jacob Viner claimed that "This formula [ie the advocacy of counter-cyclical fiscal policy] may have been a discovery of Keynes, but I used it at least as early as the summer of 1931, and I don't think I derived it from Keynes, with his journalistic writings I then had little acquaintance. The idea was then a commonplace in my academic surroundings of the time, and I cannot recall that any of my Chicago colleagues would have dissented, or that they needed to learn it from Keynes, or from me" (1964, 263). A recent review of the publications in scholarly journals between World War I and 1929 finds that the "overwhelming majority" of research favored New Deal-type government economic intervention (Rockoff 1998, 134).

12. See *A Treatise on Money* (1930, 255) concerning Keynes' acknowledgement of the use of counter-cyclical monetary policy at the Federal Reserve.

13. The actual price of investment capital could be "low" or "high" depending on the prevailing monetary policy and many other factors. The characterization of the price of investment capital as "favorable" is intended to convey the idea that the bargaining position of firms seeking investment capital is enhanced such that this bargaining power exerts downward pressure on its price.

14. In the terminology we will employ in Chapter 2 and beyond, the firms that conduct financial intermediation will be called financial capitalist firms.

15. See Figure 12.

16. See Figure 8.

17. See Duménil and Lévy (2005) and Felix (1998) for an overview of real interest rates between 1960 and the late 1990s.

18. Chapter 4 provides some indications of this shift in perspective.

NOTES TO CHAPTER TWO

1. See Crotty (1994) for a discussion of the expectations formation process of investors confronted by the necessity of making an "originative" investment decision in the face of fundamental uncertainty.

2. For example, Marxists in the class-analytic tradition of Resnick and Wolff (1987) oppose the exploitation of workers, meaning that workers produce surplus value which is appropriated by capitalist firms. Thus the rapid and stable capitalist accumulation sought by advocates of Keynesian welfare state interventionism is fueled by the exploitation of workers, and results in the extension of exploitative capitalist class relations to greater numbers of workers. As a consequence, a Marxism that condemns exploitation cannot endorse any attempt to insulate workers from the devastating effects of economic stagnation and volatility in return for exploitation on an ever larger scale (and possibly at a greater rate of exploitation as well).

3. This could include a variety of public policy initiatives regarding taxation, wages, labor discipline, regulation, infrastructure, as well as various policies to support aggregate demand (by government spending, for example).

4. In Marxian theory, productive capitalist firms derive their profit by appropriating the surplus value produced by workers. Thus the payment that productive capitalists make to secure investment capital is a distribution of some portion of the surplus value. Financial capitalist firms derive their profit by receiving a portion of this surplus value from the productive capitalist in return for providing one requisite of the production process, i.e. access to investment capital. Financial capitalist firms may also derive profit when they advance funds to other types of capitalist firms (merchant capitalist firms or other financial capitalist firms) or to other entities (such as consumers). Resnick and Wolff (1987) provide an extensive analytic framework to examine these and other interactions.

5. The Keynesian term "investment" is used throughout this book. The Keynesian term "investment" is not equivalent to the Marxian term "accumulation." "Accumulation" is defined as the purchase of additional means of production and labor power, while the Keynesian term "investment" focuses attention on the creation of physical capital only.

6. Firms that have the option of financing investment projects internally have enhanced bargaining power in the negotiation over the price of external sources of investment capital.

7. Below we will engage in a discussion of the distinction between debt and equity forms of investment capital.

8. As Chapter 3 will discuss, we consider an investment bank to be a distinctive type of financial intermediary that enables a productive capitalist firm to access investment capital by underwriting the securities of the issuing firm.

9. A financial capitalist might not intermediate the funds of other savers, but provide its own funds to a firm seeking investment capital. We set aside this possibility in the argument below.

10. For example, a bank might access funds via the discount window of the central bank.

11. Marx explains that the maximum payment made for access to investment capital would be the entire "profit"(surplus value) itself, while the minimum limit is "altogether indeterminable" (1967, 358).

12. In Resnick and Wolff's (1987) terminology, the interaction between productive and financial capitalists over the terms on which investment capital may be accessed is a form of subsumed class struggle.

13. Productive capitalist firms rely on financial capitalist firms given that, under the current assumptions, productive capitalist firms require access to external investment capital. Financial capitalist firms also rely on productive capitalist firms given that, under the current assumptions, financial capitalist firms derive their profit via the provision of investment capital to productive capitalist firms. This mutual dependence between productive and financial capitalist firms confers a cooperative dimension to their relationship.

14. Below we explicitly engage with the possibility that investment capital may be provided by financial capitalist firms via means other than loans, but this turn of phrase will suffice for the moment.

15. Among these various forces shaping the activities of the state are several considerations that relate to our analyses throughout this book. The state plays a number of roles that contribute to the viability of the overall economic system. Hence the state involves itself in a large array of activities that are required for the perpetuation of the economic system—everything from ensuring the availability of appropriately trained workers to providing the requisites for the execution of transactions. Alongside these economic concerns there is an immense variety of other considerations related to worker militancy, electoral pressures, theoretical currents animating policy debates, the entreaties of a large assortment of particular domestic and international interests, jurisdictional frictions between national and subnational levels of government, potential conflicts within any given bureaucracy (including conflict within entities that enact or supervise financial regulation) and many other factors. Many of these factors will play a role in the evolution of the New Deal.

16. See Chapter 4 for an account of some of the factors which compelled the state to adopt this course of action in the New Deal.

17. The possibility that financial capitalist firms provide investment capital to entities other than productive capitalist firms is noteworthy here. To the extent that financial capitalist firms provide funds to other entities, this improves the bargaining power of financial capitalist firms *vis-à-vis* productive capitalist firms. By the same token, the possibility that productive capitalist firms finance new investment via retained earnings, or have access to funds via other means (say via funds provided by the government) increases the bargaining power of productive capitalist firms *vis-à-vis* financial capitalist firms.

18. Differences in the tax treatment of capital provided in equity or debt form may be the consequence of the capacity of various entities to persuade the state to enact rules that privilege one form or another.

19. However, some productive capitalist firms may be too small or otherwise deemed an inappropriate candidate to issue securities publicly.

20. The following discussion is not intended as a complete list of potential responses; rather, the discussion is motivated to highlight some of the potential responses that are germane to the economic history of the period considered in subsequent chapters, and that might be most problematic from the point of view of pro-investment economic reforms (and the financial regulatory framework supporting such economic reforms).

21. For Keynesians, arbitrage in financial assets does not have the stabilizing properties of establishing the correct price reflecting underlying fundamentals (à la neoclassical economic theory). Instead, the attempt to profit from short-term price fluctuations can exacerbate price instability and thereby distort the expectations formation process (Crotty 1994).

22. Grabel (1999) quotes a useful definition of speculation devised by Nicholas Kaldor:

> "'[speculation is] the purchase (or sale) of goods with a view to re-sale (or repurchase) at a later date, where the motive behind such action is the expectation of a change in the relevant prices (. . .) and not a gain accruing through their use, or any kind of transformation effected in them or their transfer between different markets.'" (in Grabel, 1999, 1076–1077). On a more entertaining note, a Wall Street trader working during the 1920s and 1930s provides this definition:
> "Investment and speculation have been so often defined that a couple more faulty definitions should do no harm, the science of economics having reached a point where further confusion is impossible. Thus, speculation is an effort, probably unsuccessful, to run a little money into a lot. Investment is an effort, which should be successful, to prevent a lot of money from becoming a little (Schwed 171–172).

23. As the concluding chapter notes, contradictory dynamics would not disappear even if financial intermediaries were not organized as financial capitalist firms.

24. As noted above, the total funds available to provide as investment capital may exceed the savings collected from the public by the financial intermediaries, but we focus here on the funds that are intermediated.

25. The financial intermediary will endeavor to mitigate this via diversification, among other strategies.

26. An excessively cautious financial sector could deprive productive capitalist firms of investment capital.

NOTES TO CHAPTER THREE

1. The insurance provision referred to is insurance with a savings element.

2. This precludes the possibility that commercial banks might use non-deposit sources of funds. These sources of funds may be used by many types of

financial capitalists. In order to focus on the unique activity of commercial banking, we delay the examination of these types of non-depository activities common to all financial capitalists until later chapters.

3. In addition to the return earned on deposits, savers may chose this manner of holding savings because they require checking privileges, they perceive funds held as deposits as being secure, or they benefit from the relative accessibility and convenience of deposits (among other potential reasons).

4. This is a rather restrictive analysis of the activities of commercial banks; there are other forms of income that are typically incidental to commercial banking, but are outside the definitional limits imposed above (such as renting safety deposit boxes).

5. We are assuming that bank loans are not resold on secondary markets, thus generating the possibility of capital gains. In subsequent chapters we mention the financial innovation known as "securitization," which would enable bank loans to be packaged together and resold as securities.

6. New Deal Brain Trust member Raymond Moley described the importance of bank confidence in his memoir of his experiences during the banking crisis of 1933: " Woodin (Secretary of the Treasury) by his earlier experience in banking and I, by what I had learned in the preceding days and in the light of my political activity, had grasped an essential fact. We know how much of banking depended upon make-believe or, stated more conservatively, the vital part that public confidence had in assuring solvency" (Moley 1966, 171).

7. New Dealer Adolph Berle observed the inability to manage confidence in the banking system on the level of the individual bank in his speech to the New York Bankers Association: "Prior to the bank holiday, there was almost a standard gambit which inevitably worked itself out. A small bank or two or three of them would find themselves in difficulties. The Federal Reserve people and the Reconstruction Finance people were called in. They, as their first move, tried to get together the strong and responsible banking interests in that town with a view to working out a concerted course of action. In practically every case they were met with a feeling on the part of the stronger units that perhaps these weaker men had no right to be in business anyway, and that if they were allowed to go by the board, it would make for a healthier situation. But when the weaker units did go by the board, confidence was so shattered that a short time after, the non-cooperative strong units were themselves asking for assistance, and then they learned to know, as we had, that there was no such thing as a series of scattered banking units. It was one party, and everybody was invited, whether he desired the invitation or not" (1933, 7).

8. Attrition via mergers and acquisitions may be regarded more favorably by the banking sector in the sense that it does not provoke bank runs, although it presents problems of a different sort to remaining commercial banks in that it reconfigures competitive conditions by creating a competitor of a larger size.

9. When a borrower defaults entirely, there is often some collateral that can defray the loss of the principal of the loan. But it is possible that

the conditions that culminated in the inability of the borrower to meet interest payment obligations (say negative economic conditions in a given industry or region) may also depreciate the value of the collateral backing the loan. "Once a situation exists where debt payments cannot be made either by cash from operations or refinancing, so that assets have to be sold, then the requirements imposed by the debt structure can lead to a fall in the prices of assets. In a free market, the fall in asset prices can be so large that the sale of assets cannot realize the funds needed to fulfill commitments" (Minsky 1982, 383–384).

10. Corrigan provided three reasons for the "specialness" of banks: they offer transactions accounts, they transmit monetary policy, and they are a backup source of liquidity for other financial and non-financial institutions. The third of these three facets of Corrigan's argument is not considered here. Corrigan's original essay was updated in the post Glass-Steagall era (2000).

11. The partial reserve system is the traditional manner in which depository banking has been conducted. However, recently, some jurisdictions have excused depository institutions from the necessity of holding required reserves. Chapter 6 will discuss some of the ways in which depository institutions have been able to reduce and in some cases eliminate required reserves, and the capital adequacy standards that have succeeded required reserves as a preferred tool of banking regulators.

12. This is an approximation of how required reserves are created. In the United States, required reserves are generally acquired by trading among commercial banks in the Federal Funds market, rather than by holding back a portion of each new deposit. However, this approximation is employed in standard texts as an explanation of the banking process and the money multiplier.

13. Cash held on the premises of commercial banks (vault cash) is also counted as required reserves.

14. Of course, many capitalist enterprises (including non-commercial bank financial capitalist firms) may receive state support when they face a crisis. But it is rare that a private capitalist firm has access to an explicitly acknowledged and formalized mechanism through which an agency of the government (the central bank in this case) provides liquidity in times of crisis.

15. This also applies to other providers of funds to commercial banks, if I may be permitted to relax the imposed assumptions momentarily.

16. This implicit subsidy is particularly operative if the bank is perceived as "too-big-to-fail" (see below).

17. Even if a bank is rescued, it will face costs in terms of the injury to its reputation and increased regulatory scrutiny.

18. For example, see Wolfson (1994, 49–59) concerning the failure of the Franklin Nation Bank in 1974. Franklin was a relatively minor regional bank only a few years prior to its failure. However, once its aggressive growth strategies faltered, it became apparent that Franklin had created such an extensive web of difficulties that the Federal Reserve was obliged to extend it rather extensive support in the time prior to its failure.

19. This is a so-called "bought-deal," in which the underwriter assumes the risk associated with the ultimate sale of the securities. It is also possible to have a "best-effort" arrangement, in which unsold securities are returned to the issuer.

20. For example, the commissions earned via facilitating trading on secondary securities markets may all be enhanced in a context in which capital gains earnings are vigorous.

21. "American economists and bankers themselves generally accepted the orthodox theory of banking which maintained that commercial banking must be conducted separately from investment operations" (Edwards 1938, 166).

22. The term "commercial bank" was developed to refer to a financial capitalist firm that facilitated commerce by using deposits to fund short-term loans made to support the "needs of trade" (D'Arista 1993, 63–64). Much of this lending took the form of bridging the time period between the sale of goods and the receipt of payment, or the facilitation of payment for international trade. Until the Great Depression, when medium-term lending became more common on the part of commercial banks, this orientation towards short-term lending remained in force.

23. The provision of operating capital is also supportive of a pro-investment agenda, in that it frees retained earnings or inflows of funds from the sale of securities for use as investment capital.

24. Trescott's 1963 study conducted at the invitation of the American Bankers Association, *Financing American Enterprise: The Story of Commercial Banking* (1963), devotes a chapter to the role of commercial banking in the financing of productive capitalist firms between 1946 and 1960, and makes special mention of the role of commercial banks in providing investment capital to these smaller borrowers.

25. The list of concerns discussed in these Hearings appears in Benston (1990, 23–25).

26. Securities may serve as collateral for loans in commercial banks that have no connections with investment banks. However, the concern is that this activity will be more prevalent in a diversified financial capitalist firm given the conflicts of interest that may influence the banks' lending decisions.

27. See Corrigan (2000).

28. In the late 1990s, it was claimed that the conduct of monetary policy by the Federal Reserve was timed to support stock market values in a manner that came to be called the "Greenspan Put" (Parenteau, 2006). A "put" is an option to sell an asset in the future (a form of derivatives contract) that provides insurance to compensate the holder against a drop in its price.

29. In contrast, Calomiris (2000) makes the case that a long term relationship between a productive and a diversified financial capitalist firm can be advantageous to firms in need of investment capital. He argues that diversified financial capitalist firms can alter the form of financing available to the productive capitalist firm, progressing from lending directly to the firm to underwriting securities as the firm matures. To cultivate a long-term relationship, the financial capitalist firm may initially offer financing on attractive terms. However this argument assumes a long-term relationship between

the financial capitalist firm and productive capitalist firm. This likely entails the existence of significant switching costs to the productive capitalist firm, thereby reducing the productive capitalist firms' bargaining power once it has selected the diversified financial capitalist firm with which it may form a long-term relationship.

30. Hilferding argued that several years of bitter competitive struggles and vigorous technological change produced a rapid concentration of capital in Germany at that time. The creation of cartels shielded productive capitalist firms somewhat from this ruinous competition, but these mergers and acquisitions required large infusions of money capital. Faced with these exorbitant financing demands, productive capital became increasingly reliant on financial capitalist firms, particularly large banks, while at the same time financial capitalist firms became increasingly concentrated in order to mobilize more financial resources.

31. At that time, the lack of a well-developed stock market meant that finance capital often acted as shareholder in these productive capitalist firms rather than as underwriter that sold stock in these productive capitalist firms to a third party.

32. Morgan's investment banking activity originally took the form of underwriting securities to a select group of European investors, rather than acting as underwriters for public offerings made widely available. In addition, Morgan used its own funds to buy and hold securities. Hence Morgan's activities represent an older form of investment banking that gave way to new types of investment banking in the 1920s, engaged in underwriting securities for wider distribution.

33. The House of Morgan did not necessarily operate as a commercial bank. At that historical time, personal relationships and informal agreements were often sufficient to create alliances between Morgan and commercial banks. The partners of J.P. Morgan and Company owned stock (directly or indirectly) and/or had interlocking directorships in many large banks, trust companies, insurance companies and savings banks. In this manner, Morgan's was aligned with the First National Bank of New York, and by 1912, Morgan and Company and the First National Bank of New York controlled Banker's Trust, Guarantee Trust, and the National Bank of Commerce (see Kotz 1978, 36–37).

34. When the money trust was investigated by the Pujo Committee in 1912, they found that "tightly held bank control had been instrumental in bringing about large corporate mergers at the turn of the century and that these mergers had resulted in furthering the strength of the banks responsible for bringing these about."(de Saint Phalle 1985, 52) In particular, Morgan's is credited with encouraging the consolidation of the railroads and the promotion of the mergers that produced General Electric and United States Steel.

35. Gershenkron (1962) made this argument in the context of a universal banking system in Germany. See Zysman (1983); and Grabel (1997) who provides a useful overview of this literature.

36. This scenario may represent another version of a "finance-as-servant" paradigm, and would be animated by its own set of contradictory imperatives.

The historical and institutional circumstances that would enable that state to play this sort of command role have not been found in the American context, except perhaps during war-time.

NOTES TO CHAPTER FOUR

1. After the passage of the National Banking Act in 1863, there were four major banking panics (1873, 1884, 1893 and 1907), as well as numerous regional and local panics. The creation of the Federal Reserve System in 1913 was a response to this instability.

2. While supervisory agencies were entitled to exercise some discretion over granting charters, some of the factors discussed below compelled them to restrain their exercise of this discretion. (see Willis B, 197).

3. In the assessment of many who had recently emerged from the calamity of bank failures in the 1930s, free banking was associated with the promotion of all sorts of unsound and fraudulent banking practices. For example, see Hammond (1941).

4. Contemporary studies have revisited the question of whether free banking exacerbated bank failure rates. For example, see Dowd (1992), Kahn (1985), Rockoff (1974, 1975, and 1985), Rolnick and Weber (1983 and 1984).

5. See Sylla et al. (1987).

6. For example, in March 1900, the Comptroller of the Currency responded to pressure from nationally-chartered commercial banks to reduce capital requirements from $50,000 to $25,000 for commercial banks in smaller communities (so that they could compete with state-chartered commercial banks in those communities). In turn, many states lowered capital requirements below $25,000. In the six months following the Comptroller of the Currency's decision, 509 new national commercial banks were approved, which represents a 14 percent increase in the number of nationally chartered commercial banks (Fischer 1968, 192, Wheelock, 1992, 6, and author's calculation).

7. In a 1930 letter to the House Banking Committee, a New Jersey banker proclaimed that "the bank, like the church, is a community enterprise, its stock a community investment, its success a community pride. It is a community temple where the saver and the borrower meet in a home they call their own." (in Bremer 1935, 105–06).

8. See Clair and O'Driscoll (1991), and Litan (1991).

9. Bank failures during the 1920s were concentrated in agricultural areas.

10. Of course, the degree of competition among commercial banks varied in each state and even in each city in jurisdictions where unit banking was enforced.

11. O'Connor was Comptroller of the Currency between 1933 and 1938, a member of the Federal Reserve Board between 1933 and 1935, and the first vice-chairman of the Federal Deposit Insurance Corporation.

12. The increased stock market participation of the US public is credited to various factors; including the popularity of wartime Liberty Bonds and the

increasing availability of securities issued in smaller denominations (see Carrosso 1970, 249–250).

13. See D'Arista (1993, 64).

14. Currie's category of "commercial" loans is actually "all other loans," which he regards as commonly equated with commercial loans. He reports that commercial loans in the strict sense (loans eligible for rediscount) declined relative to other assets of national banks from 21.1 percent in 1923 to 13.9 percent in 1929 (Currie 1931, 698). Peach (1941) provides a similar account.

15. It consists of all the corporate securities issued, and thus it will include securities issued by firms that are not productive capitalist firms. For example, it includes securities issued by financial capitalist firms.

16. Certainly not all of these loans were made to productive capitalist firms.

17. Perkins (1971) provides a concise overview of the evolution of trust companies and their involvement in both securities markets and depository banking.

18. Commercial banks complained that their ability to provide loans to large productive capitalist firms was being thwarted by restrictions on the size of loan that could be made to an individual borrower (White 1985, 288).

19. Kaufman and Mote (1992) claim, contra many authorities in the field, that the Comptroller of the Currency issued no formal ruling in 1902 specifically prohibiting nationally-chartered commercial banks from dealing in securities. They claim that these banks could only engage in investment banking activities via the "incidental powers provision" of the National Bank Act, while state chartered commercial banks often had explicit authorization to engage in investment banking. Thus the more permissive regulatory climate enjoyed by state chartered commercial banks enhanced their ability to engage in investment banking activities, and the Mcfadden Act was demanded to equalize the status of national and state commercial banks in this respect.

20. Peach's actual terminology is "all national bank affiliates, commercial banks and trust companies."

21. Note that the return on assets must be multiplied by the so-called "equity multiplier" (a leverage factor) to derive the return on equity, a measure which is frequently used to evaluate profitability. Hence return on assets is typically a much lower number than the return on equity (see Sinkey 2002, 131).

22. Compton (1987, 11) claims that about $7 billion in deposits were lost due to bank failures in the five years prior to the passage of the Glass-Steagall Act.

23. D'Arista notes the prevalence of this problem in 1932 (1993, 163).

24. Friedman and Schwartz argue that from August of 1929 to March of 1933, the change in high-powered money should have produced a rise in the stock of money of 17.5 percent. However, a rise in the currency-deposit ratio (reflecting withdrawals of currency from bank accounts) and a rise in the excess-reserve-to-deposit ratio (reflecting increased commercial bank holding of excess reserves during a time of banking panics) produced a drop in

the money stock of 35 percent, despite the increase in high-powered money. (Friedman and Schwartz, 1963, 332–3).

25. Epstein and Ferguson state that rates on short-term Treasury notes dropped from 3.4 percent in 1929 to 0.34 percent in 1932 (1984, 970). They claim that as interest rates fell, commercial banks were unable to realize capital gains from these government securities because of the shortness of the banks' portfolios.

26. Epstein and Ferguson conclude with a remark on the dilemma faced by the Federal Reserve because it must insure that the agents of monetary policy, commercial banks, must be profitable to operate in their capacity as the transmission mechanism of monetary policy: "As Keynes alone seems to have recognized, the capitalist organization of finance implies that interest rates may fail to drop low enough to revive an economy because bank earnings might not permit it in an acute Depression. Moreover, contemporary students of money and banking have not reconciled a fundamental problem of the current system of bank regulation: that the Federal Reserve system is charged with performing two often incompatible tasks—that of advancing the interests of a specific industry while simultaneously overseeing the protection of other business and the public at a large" (1984, 982–983).

27. http://www.presidency.ucsb.edu/ws/index.php?pid=14473.

28. See Benston (1990, 29–31) for a description of the failure of the Bank of United States that disputes the proposition that the separation of commercial and investment banking could have prevented the bank's failure.

29. For example, National City Company was accused of rescuing the parent bank from the consequences of its disastrous Cuban Sugar loans by selling stocks in the failing sugar company to investors who were not apprised of the dubious quality of these stocks. The proceeds of this public offering allowed National City Bank to avoid a large loan loss (Pecora 1939, 122), but left stock-holders with next to nothing. Its questionable securities underwriting included bonds issued by borrowers that were earlier described by bank officials as "lax, negligent, and entirely uninformed about the responsibilities of a long-term borrower" (Carosso 1970, 330). National City was also suspected of manipulating copper prices to protect itself from losses on the large amount of Anaconda Copper Company stocks it held (Kotz, 1978, 51).

30. Kazakévich (1934, 556) indicate that in 1926 (prior to the passage of the McFadden Act), 30.1 percent of the loans of national banks were secured by stocks and bonds. By 1930, 37.8 percent of the loans of national banks were secured by stocks and bonds.

31. In this quotation, Willis is drawing conclusions from previous experiences with the blending of commercial and investment banking that occurred prior to the passage of the Federal Reserve Act.

32. This was to be accomplished by allowing the central bank to discount only "real bills," or credit arising from production, the financing of international trade, and associated activities (see Meltzer, 2000).

33. For example, Benston (1996, 37) provides this summary of the prevailing perception via this quotation taken from a 1981 Supreme Court ruling:

"It is familiar history that the Glass-Steagall Act was enacted in 1933 to protect bank depositors from any repetition of the wide-spread bank closings that occurred during the Great Depression. Congress was persuaded that speculative activities, partially attributable to the connection between commercial banking and investment banking, had contributed to the rash of bank failures."

34. As Benston points out, this quotation is taken from the appendix to Volcker's 1986 Congressional testimony. While Volcker referred to this appendix during his testimony, the appendix was prepared by Melanie Fein.

35. Some contributions to this literature were published after Benston's 1990 book, but are included for consideration in Benston (1996).

36. For example, White (1986) disputes the hypothesis that security affiliates' operations had deleterious effects on the soundness of banks, and Krozner and Rajan (1994) investigate the proposition that conflicts of interest between commercial and investment banking caused securities affiliates to underwrite bonds likely to default.

37. As Walter Cadette of J.P. Morgan summarized: "Many of the [Banking Act of 1933's] key features, including deposit insurance which helped immeasurably to restore a sense of confidence in the banking system, were an apposite response to the crisis. But others, including the sections that separated commercial and investment banking and became known as the Glass-Steagall Act, were not. Indeed, they were wide of the mark—the product of a hurried search for scapegoats and for readily understandable, albeit simplistic, remedies to the economic ills engulfing the nation" (1996, 710).

38. "Department store" banks earned this nickname in reference to their ability to meet all of their customers' needs. The term "department store banking "was mimicked in the 1990s, when advocates of a return to the blending of commercial and investment banking claimed that financial capitalist firms would provide a "financial supermarket" with the purported advantages of "one-stop shopping."

39. This is not to say that the diversified financial capitalist firms of 1927 represent an unambiguous return to conditions reminiscent of Hilferding's finance capital. Other factors also need to be considered (such as the possibility of productive capitalist firms relying on retained earnings rather than external financing). However, to the extent that the organizational form of the diversified financial capitalist firm creates the possibility that financial capital can maneuver into a position that compromises the bargaining power of productive capital, and thereby bid up the costs of accessing investment capital, this organizational form is an anathema to the pro-investment agenda.

NOTES TO CHAPTER FIVE

1. The Banking Act of 1933 was preceded by the Emergency Banking Act of March 9, 1933 (which proclaimed the National Banking Holiday). However that act was aimed at containing the banking crisis rather than instituting structural reforms.

2. The Glass-Steagall Act discussed below should not be confused with the earlier Glass-Steagall Act of February 1932, which instituted some amendments to the Federal Reserve Act concerning rediscounting practices at Federal Reserve banks.

3. Previous chapters have emphasized that contextual circumstances will determine whether downward pressure on the price of investment capital—in this case loans—translates into diminished profitability for banks.

4. "Because most of the individual proposals focused on increasing bank safety by decreasing competition in a particular area, the Act, taken as a whole, was blatantly anticompetitive" (Kaufman 1988,184). Benston (1990, 134–138) provides an overview of the interpretations of the Glass-Steagall Act as a restraint on competition.

5. These remarks were made during Senate hearings that were requested by leading bankers to discuss the 1932 legislation that Senator Glass had introduced to divorce commercial and investment banking. The remarks quoted above were made in reaction to the proposed legislation under review at that time. Ultimately, the Banking Act of 1933 made provisions to allow commercial banks to underwrite and deal in some government securities (see below). So vociferous was bankers' condemnation of his intended banking reforms that Glass depicted these hearings as an "organized protest" on the part of bankers (Peach, 1941, 154–155).

6. In addition to the prohibition on commercial bank entry into investment banking, banks were also to be subject to additional constraints within commercial banking. The Banking Act required that loan portfolios be scrutinized in order to prevent the allocation of bank credit for speculative purposes. Section 3(a) required that "[e]ach Federal Reserve Board shall keep itself informed of the general character and amount of the loans and investments of its member banks with a view to ascertaining whether undue use is being made of bank credit for the speculative carrying of or trading in securities, real estate, or commodities, or for any other purpose inconsistent with the maintenance of sound credit conditions." The Act goes on to say that a bank judged to be making "undue" use of bank credit in the judgment of the Federal Reserve Board could be suspended from the use of the credit facilities of the Federal Reserve System.

7. Percy Johnson, of the Chemical Bank and Trust Company of New York, testified at the Banking and Currency hearings of the US Senate that "I do not think [a guarantee should be made to bank depositors], unless we are going to guarantee all elements of society against misfortunes and evils of all kinds. Of course, if we are going to have socialistic government, then we ought to guarantee everybody against all manner of things" (in Burns 1974, 67).

8. Strictly speaking, Regulation Q was implemented by the Federal Reserve. The Banking Act of 1933 empowered the Federal Reserve to implement Regulation Q by giving it the authority to impose interest rate ceilings on time and savings deposits at member banks. In the 1935 Banking Act, the authority to apply Regulation Q ceilings and the prohibition on the payment

of interest on demand deposits were extended to all federally insured banks (Mason 1997, 26–27).

9. Benston (1964) dismisses the link between the payment of interest on demand deposits and the migration into "overly risky" banking activities.

10. Of course, interest rate controls could create difficulties for banks if they dissuade depositors from placing their savings in banks. This unintended consequence of interest rate controls emerged later in the 1960s.

11. While the cost of attracting a dollar of deposits began falling during the bank crises prior to 1933, interst rate controls contributed to stabilizing interest costs at this lower level after 1933.

12. See Burns (1974, chapter 3) for a discussion of various bankers' interventions into the debates about the merits of branch banking provides a summary of the arguments advanced both for and against branch banking.

13. Officials were directed to consider "the financial history and condition of the bank, the adequacy of its capital structure, its future earnings prospects, the general character of its management, the convenience and needs of the community to be served, and whether or not its corporate powers are consistent with the purposes of this section" (in Hammond 1941, 60–1).

14. "[N]o member bank shall be affiliated in any manner (. . .) with any corporation, association, business trust, or other similar organization engaged principally in the issue, flotation, underwriting, public sale, or distribution at wholesale or retail or through syndicate participation of stocks, bonds, debentures, notes or other securities" (in Kross 1969, 2760).

15. Section 16 prohibited commercial banks from purchasing equities and underwriting securities on their own behalf (with the exception of US Treasuries and general obligations of states and political subdivisions), section 21 prohibited investment banks from accepting deposits, and section 32 prohibited interlocking directorates between commercial and investment banks.

16. Commercial banks were entitled to underwrite and deal in Treasury securities and the general obligation bonds of state and local governments (Benston and Kaufman 1996, 9). Benston and Kaufman argue that these exemptions were permitted to ensure that government securities would be underwritten efficiently and competitively.

17. For example, J.P. Morgan's financial empire was carved into two separate companies: Morgan Stanley pursued investment banking while J.P. Morgan & Company engaged in commercial banking.

18. By constraining the securities that a commercial bank was entitled to hold, commercial banks could not buy equities in an effort to control productive capitalist or merchant capitalist firms. While this limited the formation of diversified capitalist firms, this restriction was evaded as commercial banks formed holding companies in order to control both bank and non-bank subsidiaries. In time this loophole was closed with the passage of the Bank Holding Company Act (BHCA) of 1956. The BHCA was explicitly justified as a measure "to maintain the traditional separation between banking and [commerce] in order to prevent abuses of allocation of credit" (in Hayes 1987, 49). It clearly prohibited bank holding companies from acquiring

"direct or indirect ownership or control of any voting shares of any company which is not a bank" (Krainer 2000, 17). Once this loophole in the Glass-Steagall provisions was closed, commercial banks were prevented from forming holding companies in order to establish diversified capitalist firms. Non-bank financial capitalist firms and productive capitalist firms could acquire up to 25 percent of voting shares in a bank's outstanding equity capital. However, any stake in excess of this threshold obliged the acquiring firm to become a bank holding company.

NOTES TO CHAPTER SIX

1. Within financial circles, commercial banking came to be referred to as a "3–6–3" occupation, following the reputation of bank executives for borrowing money from depositors at 3 percent, lending at 6 percent, and arriving at the golf course by 3 o'clock in the afternoon.

2. For example, Euromarkets posed a competitive threat to US banks in both the first and second phases of financial intermediation. The Eurodollar markets developed as the US balance of payments deficits in the 1960s increased the total number of US dollars held abroad. This gave European banks the opportunity to take deposits and make loans in US dollars. Non-US banks were exempt from American interest rate controls and from other regulatory restrictions, such as American standards on required reserves and the payment of FDIC premiums. Thus non-US banks had the possibility of paying more to attract deposits, while making up for this additional cost by saving on other expenses incurred by US banks. As the Eurodollar market matured, it both attracted savings away from US commercial banks and made loans to US borrowers. This practice became so widespread that the phrase "round-tripping" evolved to connote funds originating in the US that were deposited in the Eurodollar market and subsequently re-lent to US borrowers.

3. The following account of the various pressures exerted by non-banks on commercial banks leaves aside the similar difficulties experienced by Savings and Loan Associations.

4. It was particularly lucrative to find a non-bank substitute for checking accounts, since depositors needing to execute transactions were severely penalized by interest-free checking accounts during an inflationary period.

5. MMMFs evolved to hold commercial paper, bank certificates of deposits, banker's acceptances and repurchase agreements. Ironically, when a MMMF purchases certificates of deposit from commercial banks, the MMMF can be thought of as draining savings out of the bank deposits and obliging banks to access the funds via the MMMF.

6. Prior to 1970, the minimum denomination of Treasury Bills was $1,000, which was within the reach of smaller savers. But as Regulation Q ceilings became binding, government officials (and the commercial bank officials that lobbied them) noticed that savers were fleeing commercial banks to buy Treasuries. In 1970, the minimum size of Treasury bills was increased to $10,000. This change in the denomination of Treasuries was intended to support commercial banks in their quest to attract deposits, but had

the unintended effect of helping to stimulate the development of MMMFs (Gart 1994, 82).

7. In the 10 years between 1974 and 1984, the total value of MMMF shares outstanding grew from $2.4 billion to $232.2 billion.

8. Employer control of pension funds together with inadequate regulation made them a problematic vehicle for workers' savings. In the 1950s and 1960s, relatively strict vesting requirements meant that workers frequently forfeited pension contributions made on their behalf, and pension funds were often so under-funded or so heavily invested in the securities of the employer that problems in the firm sponsoring the pension fund spelled disaster for workers' pensions. The scandalous termination of the Studebaker pension plan in 1964 (see Wooten 2001) and other abuses prompted the United Auto Workers, as well as other advocates of pension reform, to push for the passage of the Employee Retirement Income Security Act (ERISA) in 1974.

9. Unless otherwise indicated, all statistics cited in this chapter are derived from the accompanying figures.

10. In addition, a defined contribution plans are attractive in that they offer transferability for mobile workers, they are convenient to redeem, and the entire return accrues to the worker.

11. Non-financial corporate business is used here as the best approximation of productive capitalist firms offered within the *Flow of Funds* categories.

12. Ideally we would wish to display checking and savings deposits, but the *Flow of Funds* categories are such that the line labeled "deposits" on Figure 13 unfortunately includes currency and time deposits such as the certificates of deposit (see below for a separate treatment of certificates of deposit), as well as our desired categories. Thus the decline in checking and savings deposits is masked by increases in time deposits.

13. See *Flow of Funds*, L119, L120 and L122.

14. Total credit market assets held by these various entities described in figure 14 excludes mutual fund shares, which may affect the total of credit market debt indirectly provided.

15. Total credit market assets of commercial banks include US government securities, municipal securities, corporate and foreign bonds, as well as total loans. They exclude any holdings of corporate equities and mutual funds.

16. In 1970, Penn Central Railroad defaulted on $83 million in commercial paper, which provoked a virtual seizing up of the commercial paper market, even for solvent borrowers (Meerschwam 1987, 86–87).

17. A line of credit is a promise to provide a loan should the potential borrower wish to have it. The fee for this stand-by arrangement is distinct from any interest income earned when and if the loan is actually provided.

18. The term "disintermediation" is often used to refer to a situation in which savings are diverted away from banks. I have chosen to avoid this term, since we are analyzing a situation in which savings are indeed intermediated, but by some type of financial intermediary other than a commercial bank.

19. A repurchase agreement is an agreement to sell and subsequently repurchase securities. In this case, the bank would sell a Treasury bill overnight to its customer, and repurchase it the following day. The repurchase would be at a rate roughly equivalent to the interest earned on the Treasury bill in the intervening period.

20. In 1980, commercial banks won the ability to extend these accounts to smaller depositors in the form of "automatic transfer savings," accounts that transferred funds from checking to interest-bearing savings accounts.

21. Retail CDs are classified as small time deposits, in contrast to large negotiable CDs (wholesale CDs) that are classified as large time deposits.

22. DIDMCA lowered reserve requirements to 12 percent on transactions accounts and 3 percent on non-transactions accounts. As of 1951, required reserves were as high as 23 percent on demand deposits (depending on the classification of the bank) and 6 percent on savings accounts. These required reserve-ratios were eroded throughout the post-war period prior to the passage of the DIDMCA (see Feinman, 1993, 587–588). By 1990, required reserves were eliminated on non-transactions accounts, and by 1992, the checking account required-reserves ratio was reduced to 10 percent.

23. Prior to 1980, banks were withdrawing from Federal Reserve membership because the Federal Reserve imposed more stringent required reserves ratios than many state-chartered, non-member banks were required to maintain. The DIDMCA established uniform reserve requirement for all commercial banks, regardless of whether or not they were members of Federal Reserve

24. This statistic is taken from a report by the Federal Reserve Bank of New York, quoted in D'Arista (1993, 137).

25. A commercial bank in need of funds will sell securities for some specified time period, with the agreement that it will repurchase them at a later date.

26. Thanks to a 1962 ruling from the Comptroller of the Currency, commercial banks were permitted to issue commercial paper. However, a struggle ensued when the Federal Reserve ruled that commercial paper constituted a time deposit in 1966. Ultimately this was resolved as commercial paper came to be issued by a bank holding company (or a non-bank subsidiary), and the funds were made available to the affiliated commercial bank when the issuer of the commercial paper purchased the bank's loans (Wolfson 1994, 178–179).

27. For example, rumors concerning the possibility that a Japanese bank would acquire Continental Illinois, or that the OCC had approached other banks to assist Continental, helped to produce a debilitating electronic bank run in May 1984.

28. At one point, the FDIC defined these funds as "volatile liabilities" (although this was later changed to the more benign-sounding "non-core liabilities"). As defined by the FDIC, volatile liabilities included large denomination time deposits (such as CDs), foreign office deposits, federal funds purchased, repurchase agreements, and other borrowings (Sinkey 2002, 435).

29. In part due to the unit banking laws in Illinois that limit the accessibility of deposits, Continental funded its growth in the late 1970s via the purchased funds markets. In 1981, "core deposits" (i.e. traditional deposits) made up

just 20 percent of the bank's total deposits, which included negotiable CDs and foreign deposits from Euromarkets (FDIC 1997, 242 and 255).

30. As Charles Partee, chair of the Federal Reserve Board of Governors committee on bank supervision, confirmed:

> "With Continental Illinois, when you get right down to it, here was a $40 billion bank with only $4 billion in deposits. The core of the bank was very, very small. They're selling CDs, getting money from the Eurodollar market, selling commercial paper from the bank holding company. It was an extreme case—but it wasn't all that unusual. Citibank has a small core too. Lots of big banks do" (in Greider 1987, 525–526).

31. Wolfson cites research illustrating that the importance of lender-of-last-resort support is reflected in the pricing dynamics of purchased funds markets. During an instance of instability in the wholesale CD market, a "two-tiering" effect took place in which banks regarded as too big to fail paid less on their CDs than did smaller banks, regardless of the profitability indicators of the bank in question (Wolfson 1994, 57). Thus the larger banks are more active in securing purchased funds than are the smaller banks. Sinkey notes that in 1985, purchased funds constituted 35 percent of the average consolidated assets of all FDIC-insured commercial banks, while the ten largest commercial banks held purchased funds equivalent to almost 60 percent of their average consolidated assets (2002,106). While the largest commercial banks diminished their reliance on purchased funds somewhat in the 1990s, (purchased funds constituted 45 percent of the average consolidated assets of the ten largest FDIC-insured commercial banks in 1999), medium and small commercial banks held respectively only 26 percent and 16 percent of their average consolidated assets as purchased funds.

32. Banks were encouraged to lend to third world countries by a ruling of the OCC in 1979. A nationally chartered commercial bank is generally subject to a 10 percent limit to loan to any one entity. The OCC determined in 1979 that the various public sector borrowers in a LDC did not have to be considered as a single entity, and thus many commercial banks that would otherwise have been in violation of the 10 percent rule were able to continue to engage in highly concentrated lending. A Senate report at that time observed that "a single US bank may have loans outstanding to 20 different public entities in Brazil, none of which individually exceeds 10 percent of the bank's capital, but which taken together may far exceed the limit, and still not be in violation of the rule" (in FDIC 1997, 204).

33. US commercial banks other than these nine major banks were much less exposed to third world debt , since their loans consisted of 116 percent of bank capital by the end of 1982 (Sachs and Huizinga 1987, 558).

34. In 1970, the 15 most heavily indebted nations had external public debts of about $18 billion, or almost 10 percent of their GNP. By 1987, these states owed $402 billion, or about 47.5 percent of their GNP (see Ferraro and Rosser 1994, 333).

35. This gave US commercial banks some time to respond to the problem. However, it created a situation in which, according to Sachs and Huizinga, "[i]ronically, during 1982–86 the debt crisis did not have a serious adverse effect on the reported current earnings of the banks, even though it called into question their very solvency" (1987, 567), By the end of 1986 the exposure of the largest US banks to LDC debtors was 154 percent of capital (ibid., 558). In 1987 the situation could be publicly acknowledged, as was symbolized by Citicorp's announcement that it would increase its loan loss reserve by $3 billion to address its third world debt exposure. As a result of losses connected to the third world debt problem, large commercial banks posted losses of about $10 billion in the second quarter of 1987 (ibid., 570).

36. This was facilitated, in part, by legal changes such as The Economic Recovery Tax Act of 1981 that accelerated depreciation allowances, made real estate investment more attractive, and included other provisions that facilitated the use of debt to finance corporate takeovers and leveraged buyouts (Wolfson 1994, 109–112). Many of these provisions were subsequently repealed by the Tax Reform Act of 1986, which contributed to the collapse of the commercial real estate market in the later 1980s.

37. An account of the erosion in loan underwriting standards during the commercial real estate boom in the 1980s is given in the FDIC's *History of the Eighties- Lessons for the Future: An Examination of the Banking Crises of the 1980s and Early 1990s* (1997). Overall returns on commercial real estate properties fell from 18.1 percent in 1980 to a negative 6.1 percent, and remained negative or close to zero until 1994 (150).

38. As was noted above, lines of credit ironically enabled non-banks to create the "parallel banking system" via the commercial paper market.

39. Some notional amount will serve as the reference point from which the contract pay-out is calculated, but this amount is never exchanged under this type of contract.

40. "Matched trading" (or offsetting contracts in swaps transactions) means that, for example, a derivatives contract that requires the derivatives dealer to pay the counterparty if interest rates go up will be "matched" against another derivative that pays the derivatives dealer in the same event.

41. Derivatives traded in organized futures exchanges have a clearing house guarantee to mitigate credit risk (Edwards and Mishkin 1995, 15).

42. For example, at the time of its failure, Long Term Capital Management was reported to hold $1.25 trillion of notional exposure in derivatives with an estimated value of $125 billion, despite its own capital base being a mere $2.2 billion (Mehrling 1998, 9).

43. By 1992, the seven largest US banks accounted for more than 90 percent of all derivatives contracts held by US banks (Edwards and Mishkin 1995, 14).

44. While the FDIC attempted to ban this practice in 1984 (by instituting an insurance limit of $100,000 per broker), this was defeated in court. After a protracted struggle, limits on brokered deposits were included in the Federal Deposit Insurance Corporation Improvement Act (FDICIA) of 1991.

45. Risk-based deposit insurance premiums were intended to enhance the capacity of the FDIC to handle the expenses of bail-outs, and to act as a disincentive for commercial banks to engage in riskier activities. However, this regulation has favored large well-capitalized banks that were highly rated by banking supervisors. Moreover, during the many years in which the Deposit Insurance Fund was above a given level, large banks have been freed of the necessity of paying any deposit insurance premiums.

46. By transferring default risk to third parties, credit derivatives create the possibility that a crisis in the commercial banking system may be transferred into a crisis among the counterparties in credit derivatives. For example, if insurance companies act as counterparties in credit derivatives, the Federal Reserve could be faced with a commercial banking crisis that manifests itself as turmoil among insurance companies.

47. General Electric and other firms had finance companies that predated the developments in the commercial paper market during the 1970s, but they were much less important in earlier times.

48. Even commercial banks sought to establish non-bank banks.

49. The CEBA obliged the companies affiliated with non-bank banks to face the same regulations as bank holding companies. Although existing non-bank banks were grandfathered, their asset growth was limited to 7 percent annually and the creation of new non-bank banks was prohibited for one year (Gart 1994, 88–89).

50. Subject to some restrictions, such as the requirement that total holdings cannot exceed $6 billion or 30 percent of Tier 1 capital without Federal Reserve approval.

51. The Act stipulates only that such investments can be "held for a period of time to enable the sale or disposition thereof on a reasonable basis consistent with the financial viability of the [investment]" (Kroszner 2000, 1).

NOTES TO THE CONCLUSION

1. This point is acknowledged by Kane in his account of the "regulatory dialectic" (1981, 355).

2. Within a given theoretical tradition, criteria may exist to declare some outcome "efficient," "fair," etc. For example, neoclassical economic theory provides a means of defining and then assessing efficiency. But if one does not accept the theoretical preconditions of this neoclassical definition, no trans-theoretical assessment of efficiency can be agreed upon.

Bibliography

Alexander, Kern, Tahul Dhumale and John Eatwell. 2006. *Global Governance of Financial Systems: The International Regulation of Systemic Risk*. Oxford: Oxford University Press.

Alhadeff, David. 1962. "A Reconsideration of Restrictions on Bank Entry." *The Quarterly Journal of Economics* 76 (2): 246–263.

Angermueller, Hans. 1987. "The Customer is Always Right: The Case for Functional Regulation of Financial Services." In *Merging Commercial and Investment Banking*, ed. Federal Reserve Bank of Chicago, 1–10. Chicago: Federal Reserve Bank of Chicago.

Atkinson, Glen and Theodore Oleson Jr. 1998. "Commons and Keynes: Their Assault on Laissez Faire." *Journal of Economic Issues* 32(4): 1019–1030.

Baker, Dean, Gerald Epstein and Robert Pollin eds. 1998. Globalization and Progressive Economic Policy. Cambridge: Cambridge University Press.

Bello, Walden, Nicola Bullard and Kamal Malhotra. 2000. *Global Finance: New Thinking on Regulating Speculative Capital Markets*. New York: Zed Books.

Benston, George and George Kaufman. 1997. "Commercial Banking and Securities Activities: A Survey of the Risks and Returns." In *The Financial Services Revolution*, ed. Clifford Kirsch, 485–504: 3–28. Chicago: Irwin Professional Publishing.

Benston, George. 1964. "Interest Payments on Demand Deposits and Bank Investment Behavior." *The Journal of Political Economy*. October 72 (5): 431–449.

———. 1990. *The Separation of Commercial and Investment Banking: The Glass-Steagall Act Revisited and Reconsidered*. New York: Oxford University Press.

———. 1996. "The Origins of and Justification for the Glass-Steagall Act." In *Universal Banking: Financial System Design Reconsidered*, eds. Anthony Saunders and Walter Ingo, 31–69. Chicago: Irwin.

Berle, Adolph. 1933. *The Future of American Banking*. Lake George, New York: New York State Bankers Association.

Bernstein, Barton. 1967. "The New Deal: Conservative Achievements of Liberal Reform." In *Towards a New Past: Dissenting Essays American History*, ed. Barton Bernstein. New York: Random House.

Blackburn, Robin. 2006. "Finance and the Fourth Dimension." *New Left Review* 39: (May-June).

Board of Governors of the Federal Reserve System. 1943. *Banking and Monetary Statistics.* Washington: Federal Reserve.

Bradford, Terri, Matt Davies, and Stuart Weiner. 2003. *Nonbanks in the Payments System.* Federal Reserve Bank of Kansas City. http://www.kc.frb.org/FRFS/NonBankPaper.pdf (accessed July 31, 2003).

Bremer, Cornelius. 1935. *American Bank Failures.* New York: Columbia University Press.

Buffet, Warren. 2002. "Chairman's Letter." *Annual Report of Berkshire Hathaway Inc.* http://www.berkshirehathaway.com/2002ar/2002ar.pdf (accessed February 20, 2007)

Burns, Helen. 1974. *The American Banking Community and the New Deal Banking Reforms, 1933–1935.* Westport Connecticut: Greenwood Press.

Cabral dos Santos, João. 1996. "Glass-Steagall and the Regulatory Dialectic." *Economic Commentary* Federal Reserve Bank of Cleveland. http://ideas.repec.org/a/fip/fedcec/y1996ifeb15.html (accessed February 21, 2007).

Cadette, Walter. 1996. "Universal Banking: A U.S. Perspective." In *Universal Banking: Financial System Design Reconsidered,* eds. Anthony Saunders and Walter Ingo, 696–715. Chicago: Irwin.

Calomiris, Charles. 2000. U.S. Bank Deregulation in Historical Perspective. Cambridge: Cambridge University Press. Carosso, Vincent. 1970. *Investment Banking in America: A History.* Cambridge: Harvard University Press.

Chapman, John. 1934. "Branch Banking." In The Banking Situation: American Post-War Problems and Developments, eds. Parker Willis and John Chapman, 394-424. New York: Columbia University Press.

Clair, Robert and Gerald O'Driscoll. 1991. *Learning From One Another: The U.S. and European Banking Experience,* Research Paper no. 9108, Federal Reserve Bank of Dallas (May).

Compton, Eric. 1983. *Inside Commercial Banking.* New York: Wiley.

Congressional Budget Office. 1994. *The Changing Business of Banking: A Study of Failed Banks from 1987 to 1992.* Washington, DC: Congressional Budget Office.

Corrigan, E. Gerald. 1982. "Are Banks Special?" *Annual Report: Federal Reserve Bank of Minneapolis.* Minneapolis: Federal Reserve Bank of Minneapolis.

———. 2000. "Are Banks Special?: A Revisitation." *The Region, Federal Reserve Bank of Minneapolis.* http://woodrow.mpls.frb.fed.us/pubs/region/00–03/corrigan.cfm (accessed November 20, 2006).

Cox, Albert. 1969. "Review of 'The Regulation of Deposit Interest Rates' by Charles F. Haywood, Charles M. Linke." *The Journal of Finance,* 24(1): 150–152.

Crotty, James. 1994. "Are Keynesian Uncertainty and Macrotheory Incompatible? Conventional Decision Making, Institutional Structures and Conditional Stability in Keynesian Macromodels," in *New Perspectives in Monetary Macroeconomics: Explorations in the Tradition of P. Hyman Minsky,* eds. Gary Dymski and Robert Pollin, 105–142. Ann Arbor: University of Michigan Press.

———. 1999. "Was Keynes a Corporatist? Keynes' Radical Views on Industrial Policy and Macro Policy in the 1920s." *Journal of Economic Issues* 33: 555–577.

Currie, Lauchlin. 1931. "The Decline of the Commercial Loan" *The Quarterly Journal of Economics* 45 (4): 698–709.

D'Arista, Jane. 1993. *The Evolution of US Finance* Volume Two Armonk, New York: M.E. Sharpe, Inc.

———. 2000. "Reforming International Financial Architecture" in *Challenge,* (May).

D'Arista, Jane and Tom Schlesinger. 1997. "The Emerging Parallel Banking System." In *The Financial Services Revolution,* ed. Clifford Kirsch, 485–504. Chicago: Irwin Professional Publishing.

———. 1993. "The Parallel Banking System." In *Transforming the US Financial System,* eds. Gary Dymski, Gerald Epstein and Robert Pollin, 157–199. Armonk: M.E. Sharpe, Inc.

de Saint Phalle, Thibaut. 1985. *The Federal Reserve: An Intentional Mystery.* New York: Praeger.

Dowd, Kevin. 1992. *The Experience of Free Banking.* London: Routledge.

Duménil, Gérard and Dominique Lévy. 2005. "Costs and benefits of Neoliberalism: A Class Analysis." In *Financialization and the World Economy,* ed. Gerald Epstein. Northampton, MA: Edward Elgar.

Duncan, Martha and Walter Ashby, Pat Cowherd, Eric Dahlstrom II, Kathleen Frantum, Diane Geeslin Bunch, Greg Haag, Philip Robertson, and Margo Stanley Roan, Gregory Watson. 2003. *The Root Causes of Bank Failures.* Federal Deposit Insurance Corporation. http://www.swgsb.org/fdic/fdic1.pdf (accessed April 20, 2004).

Dymski, Gary and Robert Pollin, eds. 1994. New Perspectives in Monetary Macroeconomics: Explorations in the Tradition of Hyman P. Minsky. Ann Arbor: University of Michigan Press.

Eatwell, John and Lance Taylor. 2000. *Global Finance at Risk: The Case for International Regulation.* New York: The New Press.

Eatwell, John and Lance Taylor, eds 2002. *International Capital Markets: Systems in Transition.* New York: Oxford University Press.

Edwards, Franklin and Frederic Mishkin. 1995. *The Decline Of Traditional Banking: Implications For Financial Stability And Regulatory Policy.* Cambridge: National Bureau of Economic Research, Working Paper No. 4993.

Edwards, George. 1938. *The Evolution of Finance Capitalism.* New York: Longmans, Green and Co. New York.

Eichengreen, Barry. 1994. *International Monetary Arrangements for the 21ˢᵗ Century.* Brookings Institution Press.

———. 2006. *Global Imbalances and the Lessons of Bretton Woods.* Cambridge, M.I.T. Press.

England, Catherine. (undated) "Banking on Free Markets," *The Cato Review of Business & Government.* http://www.cato.org/pubs/regulation/reg18n2b.html (accessed February 18, 2007)

Epstein, Gerald. ed. 2005. *Financialization and the World Economy.* Northampton, MA: Edward Elgar.

Epstein, Gerald and Thomas Ferguson. 1984. "Monetary Policy, Loan Liquidations and Industrial Conflict: The Federal Reserve and the Open Market Operations of 1932." *The Journal of Economic History* 44: 957–983.

Feinman, Joshua. 1993. "Reserve Requirements: History, Current Practice and Potential Reform." *Federal Reserve Bulletin*, (June) 569–89.

Federal Deposit Insurance Corporation. 1998. *A Brief History of Deposit Insurance in the United States.* http://www.fdic.gov/bank/historical/brief/brhist.pdf (accessed February 21, 2007).

———. *Historical Statistics on Banking.* http://www2.fdic.gov/hsob/SelectRpt. asp?EntryTyp=10 (accessed November 5, 2006).

———. *History of the Eighties- Lessons for the Future: An Examination of the Banking Crises of the 1980s and Early 1990.* Washington D.C., December 1997. http://www.fdic.gov/bank/historical/history/ (accessed February 21, 2007).

Federal Reserve. *Flow of Funds Accounts of the United States, Annual Flows and Outstandings.* http://www.federalreserve.gov/releases/z1/current/data.htm (accessed November 20, 2006).

Felix, David. 1998. "Asia and the Crisis of Financial Globalization." In *Globalization and Progressive Economic Policy,* eds. Dean Baker, Gerald Epstein and Robert Pollin. Cambridge: Cambridge University Press.

Ferraro, Vincent and Melissa Rosser. 1994. "Global Debt and Third World Development." in *World Security: Challenges for a New Century,* eds. Micheal Klare and Daniel Thomas, 332–355. New York: St. Martin's Press.

Fischer, Gerald. 1968. *American Banking Structure.* New York: Columbia University Press.

Frankel, Tamar. 1997. "Securitization of Loans: Asset-Backed Securities and Structured Financing." In *The Financial Services Revolution,* ed. Clifford Kirsch, 215–233. Chicago: Irwin Professional Publishing.

Friedman, Milton and Anna Schwartz. 1963. *A Monetary History of the United States 1867–1960.* Princeton: Princeton University Press.

Fusfeld, Daniel. 1956. *The Economic Thought of Franklin D. Roosevelt and the Origins Of The New Deal.* New York: Columbia University Press.

Galbraith, John. 1955. *The Great Crash.* Boston: Houghton Mifflin.

Gart, Alan. 1994. *Regulation, Deregulation, Reregulation: The Future of the Banking, Insurance and Securities Industries.* New York: John Wilely and Sons Inc.

Gerschenkron, Alexander. 1962. *Economic Backwardness in Historical Perspective.* Cambridge: Bellknop Press of Harvard University Press.

Glass, Carter. "Stock Gambling" New York Times, August 21, 1929.

Grabel, Ilene. 1997. "Savings, Investment and Functional Efficiency: A Comparative Examination of National Financial Complexes." In *The Macroeconomics of Finance, Saving, and Investment,* ed. Robert Pollin. Ann Arbor, MI: University of Michigan Press.

———. 1999. "Speculation." In *Encyclopedia of Political Economy,* (Volume Two). ed. Phillip O'Hara, 1076–1079. New York: Routledge.

Greenspan, Alan. 1999. Financial Derivatives. Remarks made to the Futures Industry Association, Boca Raton, Florida, March 19, 1999. http://www.

federalreserve.gov/Boarddocs/speeches/1999/19990319.htm (accessed March 2, 2007).

Greer, Thomas. 1958. *What Roosevelt Thought: The Social and Political Ideas of Franklin D. Roosevelt*. East Lansing: Michigan State University Press.

Greenspan, Alan. 1998. *Our Banking History*. Remarks made to the Annual Meeting and Conference of the Conference of State Bank Supervisors, Nashville, Tennessee. May 2, 1998. http://www.federalreserve.gov/boarddocs/speeches/1998/19980502.htm (accessed February 22, 2007).

Grieder, William. 1987. *Secrets of the Temple: How the Federal Reserve Runs the Country*. New York: Simon and Schuster.

Hammond, Bray. 1941. "Historical Introduction." In *Banking Studies,* ed. Members of the Staff of the Board of Governors of the Federal Reserve System, 39–64. Baltimore: Waverly Press.

Hayes, Samuel. 1987. "Introduction." In *Wall Street and Regulation,* ed. Samuel Hayes, 1–6. Boston: Harvard Business School Press.

Haywood, Charles and Charles Linke. 1968. *The Regulation of Deposit Interest Rates*. Chicago: Association of Reserve City Bankers.

Hegel, Georg. 1977. *Phenomenology of Spirit*. Trans. A.V. Miller. Oxford: Clarendon Press.

Henwood, Doug. 1998. Wall Street: How It Works and For Whom. New York: Verso.

Hilferding, Rudolf. 1981. *Finance Capital: A Study of The Latest Phase Of Capitalist Development*. Boston: Routledge and Kegan.

Helleiner, Eric. 1994. *States and the Reemergence of Global Finance*. Ithaca: Cornell University Press.

Humphries, Hubert. 1970. *The Political Philosophy of the New Deal*. Baton Rouge: Louisiana State University Press.

Hyman, Sidney. 1976. *Marriner S. Eccles: Private Entrepreneur and Public Servant*. Stanford: Graduate School of Business, Stanford University.

Isenberg, Dorene. 2000. "The Political Economy of Financial Reform: The Origins of the US Deregulation of 1980 and 1982." In *Capitalism, Socialism, and Radical Political Economy,* ed. Robert Pollin, 247–269. Northampton, MA: Edward Elgar.

Kahn, James. 1985. "Another Look at Free Banking in the United States." *American Economic Review* 75 (4): 881–885.

Kahn, Richard. 1931. "The Relation of Home Investment to Unemployment" *Economics Journal* 41(2): 93–98.

Kane, Edward.. 1977. Good Intentions and Unintended Evil. *Journal of Money, Credit & Banking,* Part 1, Vol. 9, Issue 1: 55–69.

———. 1981. "Accelerating Inflation, Technological Innovation, and the Decreasing Effectiveness of Banking Regulation." *Journal of Finance* 36, (2): 355–67.

Kaufman, George. 1988. "Securities Activities of Commercial Banks: Recent Changes in the Economic and Legal Environments," in *Journal of Financial Services Research,* 1, (2): 183–199.

Kaufman, George and Larry Mote. 1992. "Commercial Bank Securities Activities: What Really Happened in 1902: Note." *Journal of Money, Credit and Banking* 24: 370–374.

Kazakévich. V.D. 1934. "The Balance Sheet Situation." In The Banking Situation: American Post-War Problems and Developments, eds. Parker Willis and John Chapman, 548-584. New York: Columbia University Press.

Kennedy, Susan. 1973. *The Banking Crisis of 1933.* Kentucky: University of Kentucky Press.

Keynes, John Maynard. 1930. *A Treatise on Money* (Volume Two). Edinburgh: R.&R. Clark.

———. 1933. *The Means to Prosperity.* London: MacMillan and Co.

———. 1969. "An Open Letter to President Roosevelt by John Maynard Keynes, December 31, 1933." In *Documentary History of Banking and Currency in the United States* (Volume Four), ed. Herman Krooss, 2786-2788. New York: McGraw Hill.

———. 1973. *The General Theory of Employment, Interest and Money.* Cambridge: Cambridge University Press.

Kimpel, John. 1997. "Mutual Fund Investments in Participant-Directed Retirement Plans." In *The Financial Services Revolution,* ed. Clifford Kirsch, 255-273. Chicago: Irwin Professional Publishing.

Klebaner, Benjamin. 1990. *American Commercial Banking: A History.* Boston: Twayne Publishers.

———. 1974. *Commercial Banking in the United States: A History.* Illinois: The Dryden Press.

Kotz, David. 1978. *Bank Control of Large Corporations in the United States.* Berkeley: University of California Press.

Krainer, John. 2000. "The Separation of Banking and Commerce," *Economic Review.* Federal Reserve Bank of San Francisco: 15- 24. http//www.frbsf.org/econrsrch/econrev/2000/article2.pdf (accessed October 15, 2006)

Krooss, Herman. 1969. *Documentary History of Banking and Currency in the United States* (Volume Four). New York: McGraw Hill.

Krooss, Herman and Martin Blyn. 1971. *A History of Financial Intermediaries.* New York: Random House.

Kroszner, Randall. 2000. "The Legacy of the Separation of Banking and Commerce Continues in Gramm-Leach-Bliley." *The Region,* (June). http://www.minneapolisfed.org/pubs/region/00–06/kroszner.cfm (accessed March 5, 2007).

Kroszner, Randall and Raghurum Rajan. 1994. "Is the Glass Steagall Act Justified? A Study of the U.S. Experience with Universal Banking Before 1933. *American Economic Review,* 83(4): 810–832.

Krugman, Paul. 1999. The Return of Depression Era Economics. New York: W.W. Norton.

Litan, Robert E. 1991. "Could Broader Powers—Geographic and Product—Have Saved the Banks?" in *Reforming the American Banking System,* eds Richard Herring and Ashish Shah, 18–40. Proceedings of a Conference Sponsored by the Wharton Financial Institutions Center.

Markham, Jerry. 2002. *A Financial History of the United States* (Volume Two). Armonk, New York: M.E. Sharpe.

Marx, Karl. 1967. *Capital* (Volumes One and Three). New York: International Publishers.

Mason, James Elliot. 1997. *The Transformation of Commercial Banking in the United States, 1956–1991.* New York: Garland Publishing, Inc.

Mayer, Martin. 2001. *The Fed.* New York: Penguin Books.

———. 1997. *The Bankers: The Next Generation.* New York: Truman Talley Books/Plume.

Mayer, Thomas, James Duesenberry and Robert Aliber. 1984. *Money Banking and the Economy,* 2nd ed. New York: W.W. Norton And Company.

Meerschwam, David. 1987. "Breaking Relationships: The Advent of Price Banking in the United States." In *Wall Street and Regulation,* ed. Samuel Hayes, 63–96. Boston: Harvard Business School Press.

Mehrling, Perry. 1998. "Minsky, Modern Finance and the Case of Long Term Capital Management." Presentation at the conference *"The Legacy of Hyman P. Minsky,"* December 11–12, 1998 at The University of Bergamo, Italy.

Meltzer, Allan. 2000. *Lessons from the Early History of the Federal Reserve* (Presidential Address to International Atlantic Economic Society Munich March 17, 2000) http://www.tepper.cmu.edu/afs/andrew/gsia/meltzer/Munich.PDF (accessed January 20, 2007).

Members of the Staff of the Board of Governors of the Federal Reserve System. 1941. "Tables." In *Banking Studies,* ed. Members of the Staff of the Board of Governors of the Federal Reserve System, 417- 460. Baltimore: Waverly Press.

Minsky, Hyman. 1982a. *Can "It" Happen Again?* Armonk: M.E. Sharpe.

———. 1982b. "Debt-Deflation Processes in Today's Institutional Environment" *Banca Nazionale del Lavoro Quarterly Review* (December) 383–384.

———. 1986. *Stabilizing an Unstable Economy.* New Haven: Yale University Press.

Modigliani, Franco and Merton Miller. 1958. "The Cost of Capital, Corporate Finance, and the Theory of Investment." *American Economic Review* 48: 261–297.

Moley, Raymond. 1966. (with the assistance of Elliot A. Rosen) *The First New Deal.* New York: Harcourt Brace and Wold, Inc.

Mundell, Robert. 1962. "The Appropriate Use of Monetary and Fiscal Policy of Internal and External Stability," *IMF Staff Papers* (March) 70–79.

Myers, Margaret. 1971. *A Financial History of the United States.* New York: Columbia University Press.

O'Connor, J.F.T. 1938. *The Banking Crisis and Recovery under the Roosevelt Administration.* Chicago: Callaghan and Company.

Olson, James. 1988. *Saving Capitalism. The Reconstruction Finance Corporation and the New Deal, 1933–1940.* Princeton: Princeton University Press.

Palley, Thomas. 2006. *The Fallacy of the Revised Bretton Woods Hypothesis: Why Today's International Financial System is Unsustainable.* Public Policy Brief No. 85, (June) http://www.levy.org/default.asp?view=publications_view&pubID=10c10a9b6a5 (accessed January 20, 2007).

Peach, Nelson. 1941. *The Security Affiliates of National Banks.* Baltimore: The John Hopkins Press.

Pecora, Ferdinand. 1939. *Wall Street Under Oath.* New York: Simon and Schuster.

Perkins, Edwin. 1971. "The Divorce of Commercial and Investment Banking: A History." *The Banking Law Journal,* 88: 483–528.

Resnick, Stephen and Richard Wolff. 1987. *Knowledge and Class*. Chicago: The University of Chicago Press.

Rockoff, Hugh. 1974. "The Free Banking Era: A Reexamination." *Journal of Money, Credit and Banking* 6: 141–67.

———. 1975. *The Free Banking Era: A Reconsideration*. New York: Arno Press.

———. 1985. "New Evidence on Free Banking in the United States." *The American Economic Review* 75 (4): 886–889.

———. 1998. "By Way of Analogy: The Expansion of the Federal Government in the 1930s." In *The Defining Moment: The Great Depression and the American Economy in the Twentieth Century*, eds. Micheal Bordo, Claudia Goldin and Eugene White. Chicago: The University of Chicago Press.

Rolnick, A.J., and Weber, W.E. 1983. "New Evidence on the Free Banking Era." *American Economic Review* 73 (5): 1080–91.

———. 1984. "The Causes of Free Bank Failures." *Journal of Monetary Economics* 14: 267–91.

Roosevelt, Franklin. 1933. *First Inaugural Address*, March 4, 1933. http://www.presidency.ucsb.edu/ws/index.php?pid=14473 (accessed March 10, 2007)

———. 1966. "Bold Persistent Experimentation." In *New Deal Thought*, ed. Howard Zinn, 77–83. Indianapolis: Bobbs-Merrill.

Roussakis, Emmanuel. 1997. *Commercial Banking in an Era of Deregulation*. Westport Connecticut: Praeger Publishers.

Sachs, Jeffrey and Harry Huizinga. 1987. "U.S. Commercial Banks and the Developing-Country Debt Crisis." *Brookings Papers on Economic Activity* 2, 555–601.

Schwartz, Jordan. 1987. *Liberal: Adolph A. Berle and the Vision of an American Era*. New York: The Free Press.

Schwed, Fred. 1995. *Where are the Customers' Yachts? Or a Good Hard Look at Wall Street*. New York: J. John Wiley & Sons, Inc.

Shutt, Harry. 1998. *The Trouble with Capitalism*. New York: Zed Books.

Sinkey, Joseph. 2002. *Commercial Bank Financial Management*, 6th ed. New Jersey: Prentice Hall.

Stiglitz, Joseph E. 2003. *The Roaring Nineties: A New History of the World's Most Prosperous Decade*. New York: W.W. Norton & Company.

Stockhammer, Engelbert. 2004. "Financialization and the Slowdown of Accumulation." *Cambridge Journal of Economics* 28 (5): 719–741.

Sylla, Richard, John Legler, and John Wallis. 1987. "Banks and State Public Finance in the New Republic: The United States, 1790–1860." *Journal of Economic History* 47: 391–403.

Thomas, Norman. 1967. "The 30s as a Socialist Recalls Them." in *As We Saw The Thirties; Essays On Social And Political Movements Of A Decade*, ed. Rita James Simon, 102–122. Urbana: University of Illinois Press.

Trescott, Paul. 1963. *Financing American Enterprise: The Story of Commercial Banking*. Harper and Row.

Vietor, Richard. 1987. "Regulation-Defined Financial Markets: Fragmentation and Integration in Financial Services." In *Wall Street and Regulation*, ed. Samuel Hayes, 7–62. Boston: Harvard Business School Press.

Viner, Jacob. 1964. "Comments on My 1936 Review of Keynes' *General Theory.*" In *Keynes General Theory: Reports of Three Decades,* ed. Robert Lekachman. New York: St. Martin's Press.

Wheelock, David. 1992. *Government Policy and Banking Instability: Overbanking in the 1920s,* Federal Reserve Bank of St. Louis. Working Paper 1992–007A. http://research.stlouisfed.org/wp/1992/92–007.pdf (accessed December 31, 2006)

White, Eugene. 1982. "The Political Economy of Banking Regulation, 1864–1933." *The Journal of Economic History* 42 (1), The Tasks of Economic History, March 33–40.

———. 1985. "The Merger Movement in Banking, 1919–1933." *The Journal of Economic History* 45 (2), 285–291.

———. 1986. "Before the Glass-Steagall Act: An Analysis of the Investment Banking Activities of National Banks" *Explorations in Economic History* 23, 33–55.

Willis, Parker. 1934a. "A Crisis in American Banking." In *The Banking Situation: American Post-War Problems and Developments.* eds Parker Willis and John Chapman, 103–118. New York: Columbia University Press.

———. 1934b. "Commercial, Investment and Other Types of Banking." In *The Banking Situation: American Post-War Problems and Developments.* eds Parker Willis and John Chapman, 176–205. New York: Columbia University Press,.

Wolfson, Martin. 1994. *Financial Crisis: Understanding the Postwar US Experience,* 2nd ed. Armonk, New York: M.E. Sharpe.

———. 1994. "The Financial System and the Social Structure of Accumulations." In *Social Structures of Accumulation.* eds. David Kotz, Terrence McDonough and Michael Reich. Cambridge: Cambridge University Press.

Wooten, James. 2001. "The Most Glorious Story of Failure in the Business: The Studebaker-Packard Corporation and the Origins of ERISA." *Buffalo Law Review* 49: 683- 739.

Wyatt, Walter. 1941. "Federal Banking Legislation." In *Banking Studies,* ed. Members of the Staff of the Board of Governors of the Federal Reserve System, 39–64. Baltimore: Waverly Press.

Zysman, John. 1983. *Government, Markets and Growth: Financial Systems and the Politics of Industrial Changes.* Ithaca: Cornell University Press.

Index

Federal Reserve (central bank) *see* monetary
    policy; lender of last resort
bank failures, 117n.18, 120n.1, 131n. 46
bank regulation and, 49, 77, 100–101,
    116n. 7, 124nn. 6, 8, 128n.23,
    128n. 26
Carter Glass and, 60
concern about bank profitability, 56–57
Fidelity National Bank, 100
Finance Capital *see* Rudolph Hilferding
Finance Company, 98, 100
Finance as servant proposition
    commercial banks and, 8–9, 23, 32–33,
        35–36, 39, 66–67
    consequence for financial intermediaries,
        7–8, 19–21, 29–30
    contradictory imperatives of, 8–9, 15,
        19–21, 23, 66–68, 79–81
    defined, 19
    diversified financial capitalist firms,
        43–46, 63–64
    mutual constitutivity and, 11–13, 22–23
    price of investment capital, 7–9, 19–20,
        23, 64, 66–67
    responses by financial capitalist to, 12,
        15 20–21, 24–28
    Welfare state and, 1–3, 4
Financial Capitalist Firm *see also* commer-
    cial bank; diversified financial
    capitalist firm; finance-as-
    servant; price of investment
    capital
    activities of, 26, 31–32
    bargaining power with productive capi-
        talist firms, 24–26, 43–45, 52,
        63–67, 77–79, 102
    capital gains, 26
    categories of 31–32
    competition among, 16, 24, 30, 64, 85,
        126n. 2
    defined, 18, 113nn. 4,9
    potential responses to finance-as-servant
        agenda, 24–28
    profitability of, 20, 29
    versus productive capitalist firm, 18–19
Financial Holding Company (FHC), 101
Financial Intermediation, *see also* financial
    capitalist firm
    characteristics of financial intermediaries,
        18–19
    commercial banks, 33, 69, 79, 89, 93
    investment banks, 40

phases of, *see also* spread, 29—30, 36, 51,
    69, 77–80, 85–87, 93–94, 102
Financial Services Modernization Act
    (Gramm-Leach Bliley Act), 81,
    101
Financialization, 1, 101–102
First National Bank of Chicago, 53
Flemming, Marcus, 2
Free banking, 48–49, 73–74, 76, 120n. 3,
    120n. 4
Friedman, Milton and Anna Schwartz, 56,
    70, 80, 121n. 24

G
"Golden Age" of Welfare State, see Welfare
    State
General Electric, 86, 98, 119n. 34, 131n. 47
Glass, Carter, 49, 60, 73
Glass- Steagall Act
    as part of Banking Act of 1933, 9, 65,
        77, 112n. 8
    bank profitability, 68
    bargaining power issues, 66–67, 77–82
    Carter Glass, 49, 60, 66
    compartmentalization of finance, 4,
        10–11, 31, 67, 77–79
    conflicts of interest, 41, 66
    contradictory imperatives of, 82, 83–85
    deterrent to speculation, 47–48, 66,
        122n. 33
    finance-as-servant, 40, 67, 76–82
    Glass-Steagall Act of 1932, 124n. 2
    impacts on competition, 68, 74, 78–80,
        124n. 4
    motivated by antipathy towards finan-
        ciers, 80–81, 123n. 37
    parallels between 1920s and 1990s, 5
    repeal of, 62–63, 67, 83–85, 98–101
Government Sponsored Enterprises (GSE),
    87–89
Gramm-Leach Bliley Act *see* Financial Ser-
    vices Modernization Act
Great Depression
    challenge to economic status quo, 3, 108
    bank instability, 50, 54–61, 73, 75, 122n.
        33
    compels financial capitalists to submit to
        reforms, 21
Gulf and Western, 100

H
Hegel, Georg, 11, 20

For Product Safety Concerns and Information please contact our EU
representative GPSR@taylorandfrancis.com Taylor & Francis Verlag GmbH,
Kaufingerstraße 24, 80331 München, Germany

Printed and bound by CPI Group (UK) Ltd, Croydon, CR0 4YY
01/05/2025
01858455-0001